# The Alchemy of Fairy Tales

## Volume 1

—∞•∞—

## L. E. Wilkins

# The Alchemy of Fairy Tales
## Volume 1

*Classic Labyrinth Design*

For Michael Gleue, my husband,
Ursula Logan, my daughter, and
Callie and Campbell Logan, my granddaughters

# CONTENTS

# Acknowledgments

Deep gratitude goes to the late Gary V Hartman for gifting me with his fairy tale translations which brought a structure to the theory of transcendence and a method of bringing that theoretical framework into this accessible alchemical text. Also, to Sandra Schumm, Kim Condon, Ken Buch, Joseph Rodriguez, and David Strabala who offered constructive feedback in our writing group. In addition, wonderful encouragement came through the participants of the Fairy Tale classes that I have co-hosted and taught over 3 decades. And, to Sharon Condon for her devotion in both editing and technical support without which this book would not exist.

In addition, I am grateful for the privilege of my patients through the years who shared aspects of their soulful journeys with me. Each of their journeys have been my journey as well.

None of my work would have been possible without the love and support from my husband, Mike Gleue.

To see a World in a Grain of Sand
And a Heaven in a Wild Flower
Hold Infinity in the palm of your hand
And Eternity in an hour....William Blake

# Forward

At age eight, I drew a picture of what I grew to understand was of archetypal proportions. It was a picture of a great chamber with black and white stone tiles with a king and a queen sitting on their thrones. I now recognize such an image as an archetypal expression of divine royalty. One of the first depictions of the divine couple is found in the Rosary of the Philosophers (*Rosarium philosophorum sive pretiosissimum donum Dei*) woodcuts of a 16th-century alchemical treatise, the progression of the archetypal royalty is foundational to its methodology which

*Figure 1: Woodcut from Rosarium Philosophorum*

uses images to communicate the progression through the enlightenment journey.[1] In the *Rosarium Philosophorum*, animus and anima energies are depicted as the King and Queen on their journey toward the philosopher's gold (see Figure 1).

Many years later, in researching for this book on *The Alchemy of Fairy Tales,* I am, yet again, struck by the synchronicity of an image from my childhood finding deeper expression within Khunrath's *Amphitheatrum sapient aeternae*[2] (see Figure 2 in the Introduction). Once again, I entered into that chamber of my drawing but, this time, among the numerous alchemical symbols represented and to be referenced throughout this book, there is a chair for the alchemist who is depicted kneeling at the altar of the tabernacle found within the chamber, and there is a coat of arms representing royalty.

In Marie-Louise von Franz's book, *Number and Time*[3], she acknowledges numbers as archetypal foundations, representing pre-conscious patterns of thought common to all human psyches, therefore, constituting a method of knowledge more pure than mythological images[3]. In recognizing the vibrational energies found in numbers, the ancient alchemists' honored their relevance to alchemical processes. As such, these numerical symbols exist both in the conscious and the collective unconscious realms. Another way of saying this is, they are and they are not time bound. When the synchronistic awareness occurs within an individual, there has been a tethering within the space-time of the individual; a motion, a movement both in and out of the continuum of time.

The synchronicities continue to unfold around this Fairy Tale Project. Most were experienced initially with the analyses of the first eight Fairy Tales[4]. A wonderful surprise occurred, once I made the decision to use an alchemical image at the beginning of each section in the Introduction. The image I was initially drawn to was that of the *Amphitheatrum sapiential aeternae* (also known as the Alchemist's Laboratory) by Heinrich Conrad Khunrath of Hanau, Germany, a town also known as the city of the Brothers Grimm. This was indeed a true synchronicity, an event completely unanticipated. Synchronicity is a term used by C. G. Jung in reference to a causal or meaningful coincidence. Synchronicities originate out of the collective unconscious and aligns with purpose, where seemingly random events begin to reveal connections—that the publishing of ancient alchemical drawings, etchings, etc., originally under the ownership of King Charles I, originated in the very town and, at the same time our Brothers Grimm were collecting Fairy Tales.

I then recognized what had been occurring was a four-fold (quaternary) synchronicity. The reality was that these two things, the Grimm brothers collecting the Fairy Tales and the publishing of the ancient alchemical images, were going on in the same place, at the same time. While I was discovering the alchemical significance within a single Fairy Tale, I also recognized deep alchemical processes at work within me. Therefore, in choosing the alchemical images for the Introduction, I am illustrating the recognition of the alchemical processes present in each Fairy Tale. Being aware of the Grimm brothers' work and Khunrath's work as well as my own research, with Fairy Tales and alchemy, reveals the multidimensionality and holographic nature innate in my awareness of these synchronicities.

In order to be true to the process, with humility, I must recognize myself as an alchemist of Fairy Tales. By selecting the Fairy Tale to illustrate, each of the artists of these four Fairy Tales found in this book also entered into their own creative alchemical journeys. Actually, any of us, when following our soul's journey, have the capacity to recognize the energies of the alchemists at work within us. Mining a single Fairy Tale, whether for its artistic representations or its variety of meanings, is not unlike the ancient alchemist's attempt to discover the precious stone, the elixir of life, and the philosophical gold. Those of us who have studied Carl Jung know that the three domains studied by alchemists of old were following a template in the unconscious that Jung was able to recognize as analogous to the individuation journey of a single person. He was aware of the illusionary and projective dynamic found in the alchemist's work as referenced in Jung's quote at the beginning of chapter one.

This first book exploring the four Fairy Tales described below has been researched from both a depth psychology perspective and my five decades of clinical practice experiences. This approach of both research and application is also emphasized in the illustration, *Amphitheatrum sapient aeternae,* at the beginning of the Introduction, as it illustrates the foundational processes in alchemy and in my 21st century process of research and application.

The Fairy Tale, "Little Red Cap," is viewed from this 21st century perspective which includes recognition of transgender roles, precociousness and redemption. The second Fairy Tale, "The Seven Ravens," shows how secrets empower a family system to move away from stagnant outdated fears and enter into redemption and wholeness. The tale, "Concerning Little Bird, Little Mouse and the Bratwurst," exposes the folly of letting others determine what is best for you. Yet, due to the gullibility of the Little Bird everyone is forced into another opportunity for salvation through rebirth. The final Fairy Tale for this book, "The Frog Prince," illuminates how scapegoating is a collaborative unconscious collusion that can be overcome with the evolution of consciousness.

Lois E. Wilkins, PhD, APRN
DeSoto, Kansas
June 2020

# *INTRODUCTION*

# Guide to the Multidimensionality in Alchemy Experienced through Fairy Tales

*Figure 2   Amphitheatrum sapient aeternae*

## Experienced through Fairy Tales

I hold the view that the alchemist's hope of conjuring out of matter the philosophical gold, or the panacea, or the wonderful stone, was only in part an illusion, an effect of projection; for the rest it corresponded to certain psychic facts that are of great importance in the psychology of the *unconscious. As is shown by the texts and their symbolism, the alchemist projected what I would call the process of individuation into the phenomena of chemical change. A scientific term like "individuation" does not mean that we are dealing with something known and finally cleared up, on which there is no more to be said. It merely indicates an as yet very obscure field of research much in need of exploration: the centralizing processes in the unconscious that go to form the personality. We are dealing with life-processes which, on account of their numinous character, have from time immemorial provided the strongest incentive to the formation of symbols. These processes are steeped in mystery; they pose riddles with which the human mind will long wrestle for a solution, and perhaps in vain.*

(Jung, 1974)

Fairy Tales are holographic. The term, holographic, comes from the word hologram, which is derived from the Greek words, holos, meaning whole and gram or gramma, which means message. Therefore, a Fairy Tale produces, through the imagination in our realm of three-dimensionality, the most recognized feature of Fairy Tales or stories—the capacity to represent wholeness. Fairy Tales in their multidimensionality, provide numerous portals of entry to explore a variety of meanings determined by the reader. As such, they transcend time. A reader—or at first, a listener, as they were stories initially told in the oral traditions of all cultures—enters into each Fairy Tale with their own biases, beliefs, curiosities, and expectations. In the analyses of the Fairy Tales in this book, alchemy is used as the template for understanding their holographic multidimensionality.

For many, as seen in the quote by Jung, the intention of the alchemist was to turn lead into gold. Yet, **alchemy,** is so much more than this attempt. As the science of various vibrations, alchemy is also holographic. As such, alchemy is represented by a multitude of images. In the image at the beginning of this chapter, many representations of alchemical/vibrational sciences can be seen and will be explored through the analyses of these Fairy Tales.

For the purpose of this book, I want to call the reader's attention to significant alchemical/vibrational aspects of this engraving. First, the alchemist is kneeling at the altar in the tabernacle, providing aspects of spiritual expression to the engraving. The **chakra energies** are implied with the presence of a man, an alchemist, on his quest for enlightenment.

**Spirituality** is also referenced in the Latin quotes dispersed throughout the etching, as in, "Happy the one who follows the advice of the Lord," "Do not speak of God without enlightenment," and "When we attend strictly to our work God himself will help us." The evolution of spirituality can be recognized from the belief systems of global indigenous peoples. This evolution continues through the Age of Pisces (C. 7 BC—C.1800 AD and interface to 2012) with the three major doctrines of Islam, Judaism, and Christianity and, now, to the movement into the Age of Aquarius (c. 1800 AD — c. 4000 AD), which is less about doctrine and more about co-creation.

In addition to representing spirituality, **Sacred Geometry** is found in this ancient alchemical image with the open books on the altar of the tabernacle, inferring the vibrational energies found in numbers and form. **Numerology** is further evident in the Roman numerals on the dome of the tabernacle. **Colors** of the alchemical processes are also represented in this image; there is an abundance of black and white and, with the fire on the left, the color red is inferred. The yellowing can be seen throughout the image, as in the woodwork, the table, and the musical string instruments on the table. Vibrational energies of **Sound** are overtly represented by these musical instruments, with the hollow body of each instrument representing the feminine dynamic of a vessel and the neck/head representing the phallic male dynamic. **Masculine** energy is overtly represented by the alchemist praying at the altar, and **Feminine** energies are abundant throughout with the numerous vessels displayed. Finally, we find reference to dreams with the inscription over the doorway at the far end of the hall which reads, "While sleeping, watch!"—a clear representation of the **Imagination** and co-creation dynamics found in dreams.

Later in his life, C. G. Jung recognized and described how the alchemists were demonstrating the psychological process of individuation as stated in his quote at the beginning of this chapter. Today, we have the advantage of the psychological knowledge of the individuation process and the variety of alchemical sciences and, now, we can see how both come together in a single Fairy Tale. That is the basic thesis of this book—to show how, for Fairy Tale and depth psychology scholars, the unconscious, subtle energies represented through alchemy, cultural values, and transformational messages unite in the transcendent dynamic found in stories. As Richard Tarnas so beautifully explains his reluctant acceptance of the relevance of astrology in his book, *Cosmos and Psyche,* I have also benefitted from his scholarship and see the similarities in finding its deep relevance in Fairy Tales. In both instances, it was the connection with the scholarship of depth psychology's archetypal theories that brought about the awareness of what, on the surface, could be seen as a dissimilar convergence, that of astrology and Fairy Tales. Tarnas, seeing the relevance of cosmos to psyche and psyche to the cosmos, is analogous to my awareness of the influence of vibrational energies, both in the cosmos and in the individual. The universe *within* the individual, as represented in Fairy Tales, relates to the Self archetype found in depth psychology.

The Grimm Brothers' Fairy Tale Project is the result of a gift I received from Gary V. Hartman (1947-2017). At the end of Hartman's life, he asked me to become the steward of his Fairy Tale library and his eighty-two translations from the over 200 original Grimm Brothers' Fairy Tales. As a private practitioner of depth psychology, I enter these Fairy Tales with the following insights. As already stated, Fairy Tales are multidimensional and, for the careful reader, they can be representative of the Self as found within the human Psyche, as described by C. G. Jung. Another insight that I bring is that of the power of the imagination, which illuminates a variety of alchemical (vibratory) sciences—sacred geometry, colors, spirituality, numerology, and the chakra energy system. Because of their alchemical nature, Fairy Tales transcend time, and my time portal for entry, as well as for today's reader, is that of the 21st Century, known as the astrological Aquarian Age. Paramount to this project is my foundational grounding in depth psychology, beginning with Jung's teachings which evolved, along with his consciousness, influencing his theory development for analytical psychology over time.

For the student of depth psychology and, specifically, of Jung, there is evidence that throughout his lifetime, beginning before his school years, the unconscious was active and instructive in him. This instruction is active in *all* children; what is unique about Jung was his ability to recall and record the memories from his childhood. An example can be found when reading the first few pages of his autobiography which clearly demonstrates the quaternary structures of air, earth, fire, and water permeating his very first memories. We can also recognize through the process of dreaming that the fifth element, ether, is represented. Therefore, from this foundation of first memories and a careful reading of the rest of his autobiography, it is possible to tease out the evolution of both his theories for depth psychology (at first referred to as archetypal psychology), as well as, his own evolution of consciousness. Having studied the works of Jung chronologically, especially supported with the more recent texts available, such as *The Red Book,* as well as the writings of numerous post-Jungian practitioners and scholars, further confirmation of the importance of alchemy became relevant in this Fairy Tale study. As referenced earlier, Tarnas investigated the alchemical science of astrology. Tarnas overcame his cultural bias against the science of astrology, in part, due to Jung's work with astrology:

> I was also impressed by the high intellectual caliber of those philosophers, scientists, and writers who in one form or another had supported the astrological thesis, a group that to my surprise turned out to include many of the greatest figures of Western thought: Plato and Aristotle, Hipparchus and Ptolemy, Plotinus and Proclus, Albertus Magnus and Thomas Aquinas, Dante, Ficino, Kepler, Goethe, Yeats, Jung. (Tarnas, 2006, p. 63)

I also honor the astrological influence found in this Aquarian age. I cannot ignore my own awareness of the transcendent influence of astrology found within Fairy Tales and how they exhibit the individuation process, in some tales, with a single character's growth ("The Singing Bone") and, in others, the growth of *all* the main characters ("The Mouse, the Bird, and the Bratwurst").

The earliest analyses of Fairy Tales were simple initial impressions, such as, "Don't go walking in the woods alone," "Don't talk to strangers," "Be kind to lesser beings," "The truth will always reveal itself," and so forth. There are a variety of translations and analyses of individual Fairy Tales, each supporting and promoting the world view of the translator and analyst. For example, "Little Red Cap," to some translators, became "Little Red Riding Hood." By having the opportunity to analyze a translation of the original Grimm Tales, as is the case here with Hartman's translations, I am able to reconsider the interpretations of other translators and analysts, yet, maintain my perspective of Hartman's translations and focus on my twenty-first century analyses. If these Fairy Tales were not alchemical, my analyses of them would not be possible. The simplest, concise initial impressions continue to have relevance today yet, because of the alchemical process—a living process, their relevance transcends time. Time transcendence finds relevance in both the psychological individuation process and in the vibrational energy processes of alchemy. In this way, receiving the teachings in a Fairy Tale begins in a very concrete manner of thinking and evolves into multidimensional thinking—mimicking the evolution of consciousness.

When approaching each of Hartman's translations, it became clear, due to my cosmology of transcendent co-creation, that evidence of their value for this new age, the Age of Aquarius (2000 AD until 4160 AD), emerged. This experience of recognizing the alchemical processes (vibratory sciences) in these Fairy Tales shows the reader how these stories have remained relevant for centuries. I am aware that literature, like all myths have survived throughout history, from the ancient Sumerians forward, and find relevance today because of the power found in their alchemical nature.

In the beginning of this project, having been a student of Jung for many years and studying Fairy Tales as Dreams and Dreams as Fairy Tales for several decades, I was surprised to find the alchemical sciences active in each Fairy Tale. Even more amazing, as each Fairy Tale was analyzed, a synchronistic experience began to be recognized within the synergy of their influence upon each other. Initially, I was not drawn to the energy of the chakra system, but once that energy emerged, I could then see the relevance of the chakra influence in all of the tales. Another example was the significance of stones (sacred geometry), which did not reveal itself until the eighth Fairy Tale analysis occurred. With such awareness, I could then clearly see that sacred geometry is relevant in all the tales, providing clear evidence of "the eyes to see and the ears to hear," and by writing this book, the addition of "the mouth to speak." This has provided insight into the benefit of the arduous process of analyzing more than a single Fairy Tale.

Hartman's translations are powerful, because he did not rely on the translations that were already available but, instead, translated from German to English from the original *Grimms Fairy Tales*. Amazingly, in some cases, the addition or subtraction of a single letter, when translating, such as an "s" to the word, "servant" in **"The White Snake"** sets the stage for the entire analysis. In **"Rapunzel,"** Hartman refers to a Sorceress. Whether a protagonist is labeled a Fairy, a Witch, or a Sorceress directs the meanings to be found within a tale. "Rapunzel" provides both the wisdom of the safe, nurturing supportive, and the withholding fear-consumed elements found within the archetypal energies of the feminine. **"Little Red Cap"** when contrasted with "Little Red Riding Hood" brings forward awareness of precociousness tantamount to the loss of childhood and perhaps gender identity confusion.

## Alchemy

Alchemy is most easily understood as the science of vibrations. Vibrations that are found through the light of imagination, the structures found in sacred geometry, the energies experienced in numerology, colors, and the chakra system, and in the co-creation potentials found through spirituality. These subtle energy vibrations are necessary—from the propelling of galactic movements in the cosmos to the nano microscopic behaviors within a single cell found in all forms of nature. All of these subtle energy representations support the evolution of consciousness.

The image represented in Figure 3 shows the holographic vibrational alchemical process representing "the work phase" of the alchemical process.

Early alchemy was referred to as an occult science. The need to keep their knowledge secret directed the alchemist's need for a symbolic language that could both record their experiments and, yet, could only be replicated by a chosen few to protect and constellate the power of such knowledge. Power was in the hands of those who could know and practice these mysterious arts/sciences. Elite rulers prided themselves in having alchemists/sorcerers/astrologers who understood invisible realities. Some of these historical figures you might recognize include Nostradamus, Hypatia, Maria Prophetissa and, from the Old Testament, Abraham, Ezekiel, and Daniel.

*Figure 3: Tripus aureus*

In the Fairy Tale, "The Mouse, the Bird, and the Bratwurst," fire plays an important role of transformation not only in the cooking of the daily supper, but in the ultimate transformation—life to death—of the bird and the Mouse. The Bratwurst "played" with the fire, by swimming in and our of it on a daily basis to flavor the broth, never completely surrendering to the transformational fate, only to have his life end by being devoured by a dog.

## Imagination

The term, "imagination" originates from the word, "image." Often, the Creator is said to only communicate through imagery. Images found in our dreams, represent the voice of Psyche, the Creator. Dream imagery contains not only visual but other vibrational images by the use of sound (as in music), colors, geometric forms, and taste. Recognizing that the senses of taste, touch, hearing, smell, and sight provide the Creator methods of communicating that, unless understood metaphorically, stays in the realm of image equaling vision only. The Creator's imagery is holographic and multidimensional, therefore, it encompasses all of the senses.[1] Myths and Fairy Tales use archetypal realities through the images found in our imagination. The alchemist used symbolic images as a method of communication, both in ancient times and today. Isn't even simple algebra an example of symbolic language? So, as we recognize how alchemy, through symbolic language, is evident in our everyday experiences, we can, perhaps, not be so intimidated by the use of symbols. And yet, to put it another way, it is because of resistance to symbolic/metaphorical language, to a more evolved level of consciousness, that so many of us struggle with math and science.

Figure 4: Imagination

Imagination facilitates perceptions that allow us to live "outside the box." It pushes consciousness beyond the realm of what can be touched, tasted, heard, seen, and smelled. Not everyone in their lifetime can be open to moving beyond concrete experiences of reality, and with that acknowledgement, comes no judgment. It is simply a fact; as much a fact as those who can, and do, embrace multidimensionality should not be judged. This is just another fact supporting the multidimensionality, the capacity to live out of both the—either/or and the both/and—of the human experiences. Imagination is fueled by examples from consensual realities and by those trailblazers that see beyond consensus. In fact, with the capacity to live and think outside the box, the question emerges, is it only the human that can imagine the cosmos, or isn't it also that the cosmos can, and has, imagined the human? In Figure 4, we see both the human on the left and, on the bottom right, representation of the ancient archetypal reptilian energy of creation (snake/dragon).

How is it that Fairy Tales fuel the imagination of both the storyteller and the recipient of the story? An example of this would be the awareness of the living function found in Fairy Tales; by this I mean, the Fairy Tale's capacity to find relevance throughout the ages. The reason I claim the Fairy Tales as alchemical is because like all myths they are living stories and, by that, they have had, and will continue to have, relevance throughout time.

## Sacred Geometry

Sacred geometry involves universal patterns used in the design of everything in our reality, most often seen in sacred architecture and sacred art. In addition, cabalistic spirituality uses the sacred geometry found in the Metatron Cube (see

Figure 5: Metatron Cube

Fig. 5) as an image for the Creator. C. G. Jung, in *Aion, vol. 9-II* from *The Collected Works,* and Marie Louise von Franz in her book, *Number and Time,* speak to the psychological aspects of the energy patterns found both in numbers and form/structures (mandalas). Evidence of crop circles, Fibonacci numbers, and the patterns found in nature (sunflowers, conch shells, etc.) demonstrate the timelessness of such structures. Numerous alchemical images

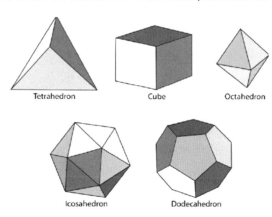

*Figure 6: The Five Platonic Solids*

depict references to sacred geometry. For our purposes, in understanding the sacred geometry embedded in Fairy Tales, we will use the five Platonic Solids (see Fig. 6) found within the metatron cube, also, the correlation between sacred geometric images and the energy vortexes, the chakras, found within an individual.

According to Renee Kryder (1990, p. 254), sacred geometry represents the alchemical processes of air, earth, fire, water and ether in the following manner. The tetrahedron represents the Fire of sacred tradition, the octahedron the Air of nature, the cube as the Earth of culture, the icosahedron The Water of the human constitution and the dodecahedron the all-encompassing Ether of spirit. The evolution of sacred geometry expressions occur in order to experience the dynamic of holography.

In the course of my clinical practice, I have worked with some people whose dream imagery initially displayed morphing geometric shapes. Once the patient and I understood some of the scared messaging provided by these images, the dreams then began to represent figures from consensual reality.

Sacred geometry uses the vibrations of both numbers and form/structure. Archetypal images could not exist without the phenomena of sacred geometry. The sacred geometry represented by Rapunzel's tower is not unlike the experience with trees. As humans, trees tower over us as they reach for the heavens. Rapunzel's tower separates her from others and places her in an aloof towering-over environment. In "The Queen Bee," we find sacred geometry in the structure of the bee's hive, with its hexagon-shaped cells, which determines the gender of the embryonic bee. Sacred geometry by its very existence bridges the mundane with the sacred world, not unlike "The Singing Bone" and the function of the bridge in this tale, bringing forth the truth.

## Numerology

The first thing to recognize about numerology is that numbers carry energy, even numbers, 2-4-6-8, carry feminine energy, or yin, and the numbers 3-5-7-9 carry masculine energy, or yang. Therefore, when we look at Fairy Tales, we are looking at the energy of numbers represented in the tale and seeking balance. The number 1 is from where all other numbers are derived. In terms of the metaphorical language of numbers and depth psychology, the number 1 can be experienced as the *number most representative of the Self.*

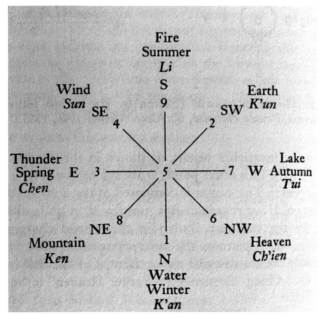

Figure 7: Pensée Chinoise

Those familiar with the I-Ching know of the predictive nature of numbers and, how, by their energy, they bring awareness of the numerical influence between the heavens and the earth. (See Figure 7)

Having identified that numbers carry the energy of either the masculine or feminine, it is important to recognize the vibratory influence of this movement. The vibration of masculine energy (3-5-7-9) is the vibration of forward movement, while the energy of the feminine (2-4-6-8) is the vibration of inward movement. It is not my intention to explore the science of numerology here. Suffice it to say that numbers are combined, and then reduced to a single digit, as you will experience later in this book through reading the Fairy Tale analyses. In all these analyses, there are a variety of ways that numerology comes through, from determining which alchemical processes are occurring in the tale to how wholeness, such as King-Queen-Son-Daughter, is or is not represented.

## Colors

Colors represent the vibratory influences of light. For the purposes of these Fairy Tale analyses, I am staying with the representation of the four phases of alchemy, although others break the alchemical processes into seven phases. The four classic alchemical processes are represented by the colors of black (*nigrado*), white (*albedo*), yellow (*citrinitas*), and red (*rubedo*). Black, the first phase, is all matter contained within the *prima materia,* therefore, all colors are represented in the *prima materia* in this phase. The second state, white, using the analogy of a seed, whether the seed of a thought, the seed of a plant, the seed of a human being in a fertilized ovum, represents death. The seed must die in order for the light of life, roots and the stem, to emerge. This is the phase when essence enters into the alchemical equation. From the darkness of the *prima materia* comes the light of life. So, in this second phase, initially recognized as a death phase, it is paradoxically also a

*Figure 8: Medieval rendition of "The Alchemy of Color"*

phase of life. The yellow, in phase three, is representative of masculine energies—solar, sulphur, which brings about the movement toward completion, which is phase four, the reddening. This would be the flowering which brings about yet another seed, so the process continues.

Wave length intervals and frequency intervals are what make up color vibrations. The black phase, the *nigrado,* represents vibrations found in chaos—energies going in all directions. In the white phase, the *albedo,* the energies have slowed and constellated to bring about new life. In the yellowing phase, the *citrinitas,* the energies are speeding up again to bring about the final phase, the red or *rubedo,* which is transformation.

In the analysis of "The Frog Prince," the golden ball takes the reader through the journey of all four phases of the alchemical process.

## Chakras

In East Indian traditions—think yoga—the chakras are understood to manifest subtle psychic energies within the body and connecting to evolving levels of consciousness, ultimately leading to enlightenment.

*Figure 9: The Chakra System*

Specifically, they represent seven psychic energy complexes that travel along the spinal column and unite with the cosmos as the sacred Self. Some who study Chakra energy systems recognize twelve, rather than seven chakras but, for the purposes of this analysis of Fairy Tales, I am going to keep my focus on the original seven. The chakra system is a recognized series of energy vortexes and consciousness found in the body. Through the practice of yoga, the awareness of transcending and tethering time emerges. With the tradition of yoga, the ultimate goal of moving beyond ego attachment (feelings) and connecting with the true Self, bringing about enlightened knowledge represented in the sacred Self. For the purposes of this book, we are focusing on the chakra systems as further acknowledgement of how individual Fairy Tales transcend time. This image is a depiction of the human chakra energy system potential.

So, therefore, we are looking at the human potential in the seven chakras system in Figure 9 on the previous page:

**The root chakra** (red) representative of Earth; survival

**The sacral chakra** (orange) Water; desire rules this energy; pleasure

**The naval chakra** (yellow) Fire; personal control

. **The heart chakra** (green) Air; compassion; love

**The throat chakra** (blue) Sound; expression; truth

**The third-eye chakra** (indigo) Intuition

**The crown chakra** (violet) transcendent connection with the cosmos

Depth psychology, through Jung's interest in Kundalini yoga, once again, shows the evolution of consciousness through the energy systems found within each individual. Each of the chakras can represent symbols from sacred geometry. As you read each Fairy Tale analysis, you will discover either a dominant representation of a chakra symbol and/or symbols from sacred geometry.

## Spirituality

Historically, spirituality permeated every aspect of life on the planet, until the time of the industrial revolution. Then, the mechanistic world view, where everything had to be concretely experienced, pushed any sense of Creator energy into the control of social systems like governments and marriage. This separation of spirit from matter was used by people in power, especially organized religion, through doctrines, to control people and keep order. As consciousness has evolved, the awareness of invisible realities through subtle energy vibrations has reclaimed the spiritual significance in all aspects of life, not just human. In Richard Powers 2018 novel, *The Overstory,* there is an awareness of the need to reclaim our connection with all of creation and not hold our humanness as having dominion over other aspects of creation.

As you can see in this illustration of "Co-Creation: Psyche's Multidimensionality," (see Figure 10) the collective unconscious is on your left, the personal unconscious is down the center, and consciousness is on the right. In the collective unconscious, you will note evidence of archetypes, the tree as healthy and in stages of compromise. Then in the personal unconscious, you will note ancient myths and stories, Fairy Tales, activation of complexes, and dreams. In consciousness, it is often through our dreams, and working with our dreams, and understanding the ancient myths and Fairy Tales that we are able to move the energy into our consciousness by allowing symbolic meanings, the animation of the trees as in, the singing of the trees. Also, growing awareness of how trees communicate with each other, both underground through their root systems and in the air with fragrances provides the human with evidence of the multidimensionality of metaphorical language throughout creation. When this awareness becomes conscious, then a choice manifests within an individual—to remain in a mundane or linear level of consciousness or to evolve into the experience of the co-creation dynamic. This experience of multidimensionality, whether conscious or unconscious, can influence, and even heal, stages of compromised archetypal energies—complexes, and this is what is represented here in this image as the healthy tree and stages of compromise within the tree.

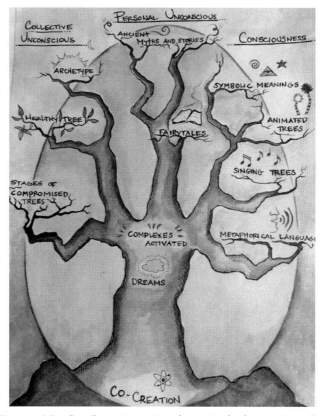

*Figure 10: Co-Creation: Psyche's Multidimensionality*

In terms of co-creation, spirituality and its evolution, is yet another way to perceive the connection between cosmos and psyche. With the evolution of human consciousness, we may also intuit the evolution of the cosmos. Where the locus of control started with humans being connected with the rocks, rivers, and trees within their ancient environment, we have an example of the internal locus of control. That was a time of enchantment. As consciousness evolved, disenchantment reigned as humans separated from the spiritual immersion in their environment, thereby, placing spirituality, in essence, into an all-knowing Father in the Heavens, an example of the external locus of control. Co-creation is the ability to honor both the internal and the external locations of control. The both/and, rather than only the polarization of the either/or spiritual existence recognizes the sacred role of individuals in the influencing of Creator consciousness. Without hubris, humanity has a sacred task of being both influenced by and influencing the Creator, which is the essence of co-creation.

## Summary

In order to understand this analysis holographically/ multidimensionally, it is important to first look at the sacred geometry (i.e., shapes and numbers) of significance in our story. In looking at the colors, the archetypal symbols, the chakras, and the spirituality, it is helpful to follow these tenets alchemical. Most simply stated, the vibrational sciences represented in the domains of sacred geometry, numerology, color, chakras, and spirituality support and promote the evolution of consciousness evident in the psychological process of individuation. Individuals perceive the influence from these symbols based on their personal vibrations. The more concretely an individual perceives a symbol, the slower their personal vibration. Some people vibrate at a frequency that allows a natural experience of the multifaceted holographic world. In order to experience the multidimensionality of the holographic world, certain vibrational frequencies are necessary. Throughout history, the trail blazers in science, art, and exploration have been said to be pulling humanity toward ever-increasing vibrational levels. Often it is believed that individuals with higher vibrations are more consciously evolved, experiencing life as infinite, not finite.

The life of Jung reflects his capacity to bring together and synthesize from a variety of disciplines, eras, cultures, etc., not unlike what we will see in each Fairy Tale analysis. The following summaries let the reader see the template provided by depth psychology through the work of Jung.

Awareness of the great diversity of the journeys explored in Fairy Tales is not unlike the numerous experiences found in all of human existence. Some can travel through a plethora of different journeys in one lifetime. Others will spend an entire lifetime on one journey. As we explore each Fairy Tale, the reader benefits from reflection on those aspects of their own lives that are revealed in each individual story. As with a dream, it is foundational to understand that a single analysis of a Fairy

Tale is completely inconclusive. The variety, the depths, and the significance of understandings experienced with each thoughtful reading may be yet another definition of a life experienced multidimensionally—holographically.

Let us now enter into the first four Fairy Tales, as first introduced in our Preface, where we will delve into the multidimensionality found in each of these tales. In **"Little Red Cap,"** the experience of precocious maturity through the loss of childhood brought into play the events of the tale. **"The Seven Ravens"** shows the significance of a single family unit growing in consciousness toward the experience of co-creating with the divine. **"Concerning the Little Mouse, the Little Bird, and the Bratwurst"** demonstrates humanity's evolving consciousness as it manifests on the shoulders of those who go first or ahead in this growth process. **"The Frog King"** provides the opportunity to explore how the dynamic of Faith are reflected throughout the tale in each of the characters.

# THE ALCHEMY OF FAIRY TALES

## *VOLUME 1*

# CHAPTER 1

## 26

# Little Red Cap

Translated from the original German version of the *Grimms Fairy Tale* collection

# 26

# Little Red Cap[1]

There was once a sweet little maid[2] whom everyone loved who even looked at her, but her grandmother loved her the most and could not stop thinking what all she should give the child. Once, she made her a present of a little cap of red velvet, and because it was so becoming to her, and she did not want to wear anything else, she was called simply, Little Red Cap. One day her mother said to her: "Come Little Red Cap, here is a piece of cake and a bottle of wine; take it over to your grandmother. She is sick and weak, and it will revive her. Off with you before it gets hot, and when you are on the way, walk nicely and properly and don't get off the path, otherwise you will fall and break the glass [bottle] and your grandmother will not get anything. And when you enter her living room,[3] do not

---

[1] **Little Red Cap** -- *Rotkåppchen*. The title is a literal translation: *Rot*, "red," *Kappe*, "cap," and the diminutive *chen*. Unlike the item of clothing from the traditional English title, "Little Red Ridinghood," "cap" covers just the head and, additionally, does not carry the quality of being hooded, hidden, or covert.

[2] **maid** -- *Dirne*. An archaic form for girl or lass. In contemporary German, though, the word is used for a prostitute or street-walker.

[3] **living room** -- *Stube*. There is no English equivalent for this room in a German house. It is something of a cross between a living room and a

forget to say, 'Good morning,' and do not go peeking into every comer."

"I will do everything well," Little Red Cap said to her mother and gave her word[4] Her grandmother, however, lived out in the woods, a half hour from the village. As Little Red Cap came to the woods, the wolf met her. Little Red Cap, though, did not know what an evil animal it was and was not afraid of him. "Good day, Little Red Cap," he said. "Thank you kindly, Wolf." -- "Where are you off to so early, Little Red Cap?" -- "To grandmother's." -- "What are you carrying under your apron?"[5] -- "Cake and wine. We baked yesterday, and weak, sick grandmother should benefit [from it] and get stronger." -- "Where does your grandmother live, Little Red Cap?" -"A good quarter of an hour farther in the woods. Her house stands under the three, large oak trees, and below it are the nut hedges,[6] as you probably know," said Little Red Cap. The wolf

---

parlor. It is the main room in farmhouses, often the only one which is heated in the winter and may well serve as the dining room as well.

[4] **gave her word** -- *gab ihr die Hand darauf* Literally the idiom means, "gave her hand on it."

[5] **apron** -- *Schürze*. Although *Schürze* does mean an apron, it also colloquially refers to "skirt." A *Schürzenjäger* is a "skirt chaser." In this double entendre, the wolf was also asking, "What do you have under your skirt?" The erotic innuendo is unmistakable.

[6] **nut hedges** -- *Nußhecken*, a literal translation. Probably hedges of hazel nut bushes.

thought to himself, "The young, tender thing is a tasty morsel[7] which will taste better than the old [woman]. You have to go about it cleverly to catch both of them." He walked next to Little Red Cap for a little while, then he said, "Little Red Cap, look at the beautiful flowers growing about. Why don't you look around? I believe, you don't even hear how sweetly the birds are singing. You are walking absorbed in yourself [8]as if you were going to school, while it is so cheerful out here[9] in the woods."

Little Red Cap opened her eyes, and when she saw how the rays of the sun danced back and forth through the trees and everywhere there were lots of beautiful flowers, she thought, "If I take grandmother a fresh bouquet, that, too, will please her. It is so early in the day, that I will still arrive in time," [and] ran from the path into the woods and searched for flowers. And when she had picked one, she had the impression that there was one even more beautiful farther on and ran after it and got deeper and deeper into the woods. The wolf, though, went straight away to the grandmother's house and knocked on the· door. "Who is out there?" -- "Little Red Cap, who brings cake and wine; open [the door]." -- "Just press on the latch," called

---

[7] **tasty morsel** -- *fetter Bissen*, "a fat bite." *Fett* suggests something delectable, not that Little Red Cap is fat or plump. *Bissen*, too, is more figurative as in "a bite to eat."

[8] **You are walking absorbed in yourself** -- *Du gehst ja für dich hin*, "you are walking all for yourself." The language suggests Little Red Cap's self-absorption and lack of connection to what is happening around her.

[9] **out here** -- *haußen*. An antiquated form of *hier außen*.

the grandmother. "I am too weak and can't get up." The wolf pressed on the latch, the door swung open, and he went without saying a word straight to the grandmother's bed and swallowed her up. Then he put her clothes on, put on her bonnet, lay himself in her bed, and pulled the curtains to.

Little Red Cap, however, had run around after flowers, and when she had so many together that she could carry no more, she remembered her grandmother again and set out on the way to her. She was surprised that the door stood open, and when she entered the parlor, she felt so strange there that she thought, "Oh, my God, how anxious I feel today, and usually I like being at grandmother's." She called, "Good morning," but received no answer. Thereupon she went to the bed and pulled back the curtains. There lay her grandmother and had her bonnet pulled low over her face and looked so strange. "Oh, Grandmother, what big ears you have!" -- "So I can better hear you."[10] -- "Oh, Grandmother, what big eyes you have!" -- "So I can better see you." -- "Oh, Grandmother, what big hands you have!"--"So I can better grab you." But Grandmother, what a dreadfully big mouth you have!" -- "So I can better gobble you up."[11] Scarcely had the wolf said that, then he made a leap out of the bed and swallowed up poor Little Red Cap.

---

[10] **So I can better hear you** -- *Daß ich dich besser hören kann*, literally, "That I can better hear you." The formulaic translation, "The better to hear you with," is somewhat contrived.

[11] **gobble you up** -- *dich besser fressen kann. Fressen* means "to eat" as animals eat, greedily, hungrily.

When the wolf had stilled his craving,[12] he laid himself again in bed, fell asleep, and began to snore deafeningly. The hunter was just passing the house and thought, "How the old woman snores. You must see if something is the matter with her." He entered the living room, and when he came to the bed, he saw that the wolf lay in it. "Do I find you here, you old sinner," he said? "I have hunted you a long time." He started to take aim with his gun, when it occurred to him that the wolf could have eaten the grandmother, and she could still be saved. He did not shoot but took scissors and began to cut open the sleeping wolf's belly. When he had made several snips, he saw the little red cap gleaming,[13] and after a few snips more, the maiden jumped out and cried, "Oh, how scared I was, how dark it was in the wolf's body!"[14] And then the old grandmother came out still alive and could hardly breathe. Little Red Cap, though, quickly fetched large stones with which she filled the wolf's body, and when he awoke, he wanted to run away. The stones, however, were so heavy that he instantly collapsed and fell dead.

---

[12] **stilled his craving** -- *sein Gelüsten gestillt hat*. The key word is *Gelüsten*, which derives from Lust, desire, hunger, or appetite in the figurative sense. The implication is that the wolf's hunger was more than just for food, another erotic implication.

[13] **gleaming** -- *leuchten*, to shine, glow, radiate. The image of something giving off light, lighting up, contrasting with the darkness Little Red Cap refers to several lines later of being in the wolf's body.

[14] **body** -- *Leib*, body or trunk. Significantly, the word is not *Bauch*,

1

Then all three were happy. The hunter drew off the wolf's pelt and went home with it. The grandmother ate the cake and drank the wine which Little Red Cap had brought and recovered again. Little Red Cap, though, thought, "As long as you live, you will never again run off the path into the wood, if your mother has forbidden it."

It is also told that once, when Little Red Cap again brought her old grandmother baked goods, another wolf addressed her and wanted to lead her away from the path. Little Red Cap was on her guard and continued straight on her way and told her grandmother that she had met the wolf, who had wished her good day, but whose look in his eyes was so fearful. "Had it not been on a public road, he would have gobbled me up." -- "Come," said her grandmother, "we will lock the door so he cannot come in." Soon thereafter, the wolf knocked and called, "Open up, Grandmother. I am Little Red Cap, I bring you baked goods." They kept silent, however, and did not open [the door]. Then the graybeard[15] crept a number of times around the house, jumped finally onto the roof, and planned to wait until Little Red Cap went home in the evening, when he would creep after her and gobble her up in the darkness. But the grandmother realized what he had in mind. Now, in front of the house stood a big stone trough. She said to the child, "Take the bucket, Little Red Cap. Yesterday, I cooked sausages, so carry the water in which they were cooked to the trough." Little

---

[15] **graybeard** -- *Graukopf,* literally, "gray-head."

Red Cap carried [water] until the big, big trough was completely full. *The* smell from the sausages wafted [up] to the wolf's nose; he sniffed and peered down, finally he stretched his neck so far, that he could no longer hold on and began to slide. So he slid down off the roof directly into the big trough and drowned. Little Red Cap, however, went happily home, and no one did anything to harm her.

*translated by Gary V. Hartman*
*© 1998 Gary V. Hartman*

*Illustration by Donna Dennis*

## Artist's Comments

Grimms' "Little Red Cap" Fairy Tale deviated quite a bit from the "Little Red Riding Hood" Fairy Tale I grew up hearing. The story of Little Red Cap was, to me, the story of my life as a child—very innocent and unknowing of the dark side of the world. I loved to be outdoors among the flowers, smelling and seeing the beauty of the landscape. Because of this, I never learned the importance of being responsible.

In my drawing, the wolf is lurking, looking over Little Red Cap's shoulder and waiting to make sure she remains in the realm of innocence before the attack. Little Red Cap is really looking forward to seeing her grandmother, but instead of doing her duty, she is distracted by the flowers. Like her, my grandmother's house was always very pleasant, with something always cooking and very joyful. When with her, I never had to think of the dark energy that was around. As I have grown up I realized that to be able to live in this world, you must know the dark side. Sometimes the innocence has to be left behind.

# #26

# Little Red Cap Commentary and Analysis

Lois Wilkins, PhD, APRN

# Commentary

This commentary will explore each of the characters found in #26 "Little Red Cap." Each character has a role of significance in promoting the timelessness, multidimensionality, and depth psychological approach in the analysis that follows.

### Title

The choice of the word **"Little"** in the title, "Little Red Cap," refers to size, age, and is also a reference to innocence (naive consciousness) and youth.

**"Red"** designates a color, representative of a fourth stage of the alchemical process. In addition, it is symbolic of blood, danger, the energy of the life force (as in the first chakra), and heat. Psychoanalytically, it is associated with sexuality, passion, and sin. From depth psychology, red is a stage of individuation where destiny has both been recognized and actualized.

**"Cap"** (found in Hartman's literal translation, footnote 1) is also recognized in other French and German translations, with the words, *"le petit chaperon rouge"* and *"Rotkäppchen,"* indicating a small head covering, *not* a hood or a hooded cape. The significance of a Cap, "crown" (recognition), when contrasted with a hooded cape/cloak (hiding or being hidden), is inferred by careful analysis of our title. Note that a Cap, in this tale, is used more for recognition, rather than for function. A literal translation of this title could be: a young innocent, full-of-life-force passion, with a crown of recognition. From this title, we are *unaware* of the gender.

## The Initial Paragraph

In the first paragraph, we are introduced to "a sweet little maid" loved by everyone who looked upon her but most loved by her grandmother. Her grandmother was [obsessed] as "she could not stop thinking what all she should give the child." One of the gifts she made and gave to her was a little cap of red velvet, which the little maid wanted to wear all the time, so much so, that she was known simply as "Little Red Cap." The significance of such a gift will direct the movement of our tale.

Little Red Cap's mother one day tells her that her grandmother is sick and weak, and she gives Little Red Cap a piece of cake and a bottle of wine to take to grandmother in order to "revive her". The grandmother lives in the forest and therefore, her mother gives Little Red Cap the following instructions, "Off with you before it gets hot, and when you are on your way, walk nicely and properly and don't get off the path, otherwise you will fall and break the glass [bottle] and your grandmother will not get anything. And, when you enter her living room do not forget to say, 'Good morning' and do not go peeking into every corner." With these instructions, awareness of the mother's knowledge of her daughter's precocious and curious nature enters into the tale.

Therefore, in this first paragraph, we are introduced to the Little Maid (Little Red Cap), her mother, and her mother's mother, Little Red Cap's grandmother. We are immersed in the maternal archetype. There is not any representation of the masculine, no father or father figure, so we know the movement of the tale will be from the feminine toward relationship with the masculine. In terms of time, we know this is morning, the time for new beginnings, "…before the sun gets too hot." We find the color red in this paragraph, through the velvet fabric of the red cap. We also see the masculine number three, finding representation in the trinity of the Grandmother/mother/child, another indication that the masculine will emerge in our tale.

The mother is aware of the needs and desires of both her mother and her daughter—the grandmother's energies of decline and the need to be revived and Little Red Cap's need to have her energies focused and contained. This awareness of the need for focus and containment of Little Red Cap's energies results in the mother's instructions of "…walk nicely and properly and don't get off the path, otherwise…you will fall and break the glass [bottle]…and your grandmother will get nothing." Furthermore, the mother promotes the use of Little Red Cap's voice by her command that she say, "Good morning" when she enters the grandmother's living room and by censoring the use of her sight (curiosity), with the instruction to not, "…go peeking into every corner." These admonishments encourage the development of responsive manners (maturing of spontaneous, instinctual reactions to the world/environment) now to be tempered with the use of cautious judgment.

## Main Characters

The **Grandmother**, in the role of wise crone, carries the energies of the magical witch (power and strength). Since it is morning in the grandmother's living room, it brings an awareness that new beginning(s) will occur in the public domain (forest/woods). See Hartman's footnote 3, **living room**, indicating this also is a public space. The red cap, made of velvet, and given to the young maid by her Grandmother (Crone), moved her from the role of an innocent child to the precocious role of one to be recognized as carrying power and wealth *beyond her years*. This precociousness was perhaps compounded by the lack of a father figure, which is further explored later in this commentary.

The **Mother** of Little Red Cap and the daughter of the grandmother is described as being in the position of knowing both what is needed by her mother and her daughter. She is in the medial space, that in-between space psychologically, as the bridge between two realities and in more modern terminology, "sandwiched" between the past and the future generations. In the first paragraph, the directives given to Little Red Cap include awareness of the use of sight ("don't go peeking into every corner"), voice (say, "Good morning"), and timing (before it gets too "hot").

**Little Red Cap**, the maiden, is introduced as "a sweet little maid whom everyone loved who even looked at her." From this description, it is inferred that she possesses beauty, as recognized in her culture, and that she is innocent. Her beauty is externally recognized. An element of shadow emerges from the use of the term "maid". In Hartman's footnote 2, "maid— *Dirne,* an archaic form for girl or lass. In contemporary German, though, the word is used for a prostitute or street-walker." This may be where the Freudian analysis of this story has taken a very different focus from my commentary and analysis of the tale. As our illustrator, Donna Dennis, notes in her comments, leaving behind innocence is necessary in order to fully embrace life. In the beginning of our tale, Little Red Cap, as a maiden, reminds us of the still-sleepy, yet heart-centered energies of innocence. It is important to note that our tale provides no evidence of playmates, either other children or creatures of the woods/forest. Recognition of Little Red Cap's lack of playfulness is an alert to the reader of her having been given the crown of maturity too soon, thereby, usurping her childhood. This false maturity is catalytic for the movement in our tale.

Missing from the first paragraph is a father or father-figure or any other representation of the masculine. Without an apparent father figure, the child's ability to be playful is repressed. Too often, the fatherless child is forced into pseudo-maturity. A serious, no-nonsense persona is often worn by such a child. The child, in order to play, must feel safe. Providing aspects of safety and security is a role of the father to provide for his children. With the feminine trinity, represented by the grandmother/mother/child, aspects from the multi-cultural awareness of healing the generations, both past and into the future, are present. We can now imagine that aspects of the masculine will appear for the healing balance in the archetype of the feminine as the trinity representation brings forth the numerology of the number three (3), the first masculine number.

## Characters and Symbolism of Images

Historically, **Cake** (sustenance) is thought to be easily enchanted and can convey both positive and negative psychic energy. Because they carry spells, Cakes became associated with rites of passage such as christenings, birthdays, and weddings. In this tale, the Cake carried by Little Red Cap to her grandmother would have been "enchanted" with the intensions of her mother, with healing energies. In this tale, Cake is recognized as an *earth* element.

**Wine** (red wine = passion) is sacred to the Greek god Dionysus, the Roman god Bacchus, and the three major Egyptian deities Osiris, Horus, and Isis. Regarded as the "blood of the vine," Wine is thought to contain a living spiritual presence that encourages harmony with nature and divine love. The royal cupbearer was always considered one of the most important members of the medieval court, and Wine became part of the sacraments of many religions. Nearly every monastery or mission ever built had its own vineyard that produced Wine for the spiritual use of its members. In this tale, the connection with the Christian ritual of communion, the body and the blood, is inferred as having healing properties. Here, Wine carries the element of *fire*.

The **Bottle** in our tale holds the wine prepared by the mother, infused with the energies of strength and healing. As a symbol, the Bottle can be representative of trapped feelings and/or the need to release the spirit and is also seen as a phallic symbol, which is yet another example of the feminine carrying the symbolic energy of the masculine. The Bottle also represents the alchemical vessel of containment for transformations facilitated by heat.

With **Living Room,** some word play is needed here to understand the Grimms use of the term "Living Room." As such, it is a room for living, not dying. It is a public room, whereas the other rooms of the house are more private for sleeping, cooking, etc. Little Red Cap's mother admonishes her, "Don't go peeking into every corner" of her grandmother's Living Room, an attempt to reign in Little Red Cap's known curiosity. In other words, Little Red Cap's mother is aware of her precocious tendencies, hence, the admonishment.

The **Path** in the **Woods/Forest** provides direction for the manifestation of destiny. The Woods/Forest represents the unconscious in its wild, unpredictable, uncultivated nature. In analytical psychology, the Forest represents femininity, an unexplored realm full of the unknown. It stands for the unconscious and its mysteries. The Forest holds a great connection with the symbolism of the mother, as it is a place where life thrives. It functions as a symbol of going into the unconscious aspects of ourselves to make them conscious. This entry into the dark, unknown parts of ourselves is common in most Fairy Tales and is represented by enchanted Forests, fierce animals, deep oceans, deserts, wildernesses, and wastelands, among others. In our tale, Little Red Cap enters into the Woods/Forest at the request of her mother in service of her grandmother's needs. This journey into Little Red Cap's unconscious provides the necessary lessons for her evolution and for promoting and sustaining the multidimensionality of the archetype of the feminine.

**Wolf #1** provides lessons related to trust, i.e., "Wolf in sheep's [grandmother's] clothing." By putting on the clothing of the grandmother, gender issues re-emerge from our title, as the title does not designate gender, leaving it ambiguous. In this early portion of the tale, we have an adolescent cross-dressing/transgender Wolf. Adolescence is a time in the psychological and biological evolution of exploring sexuality/gender roles. Later in the tale, an old grey Wolf appears. This interpretation of sexual confusion is no more of a stretch, in the analysis of our tale, than the more feminist or Freudian views of seduction, rape, and pregnancy that have often been assigned to other interpretations of this tale.

In our tale, Little Red Cap *recognizes* the Wolf that she encounters along the path. She returns his greeting to her, "Thank you kindly, Wolf". This greeting contradicts the often-used admonishment in other analyses of versions of this tale, "Don't talk to strangers." In our tale, this Wolf is *not* a stranger. The Wolf's questioning of Little Red Cap and her innocent responses show the reader a degree of her ignorance/innocence:

"Where are you off to so early...?" Wolf #1 asks.

Her reply, "To grandmother's."

Again, he asks, "What are you carrying under your apron?"

Her response, "Cake and wine. We baked yesterday, and weak, sick, grandmother should benefit [from it] and get stronger."

Next, he asks, "Where does your grandmother live...?"

Little Red Cap's reply, "A quarter of an hour farther in the woods. Her house stands under the three, large oak trees, and below it are the nut hedges [hazelnuts, see Hartman's footnote 6] *as you probably already know,...*"

Once again, from our tale, we are aware that she knows more about this Wolf than she could possibly know of a stranger.

**Hazelnuts** are known to symbolize wisdom in many forms. A Celtic myth concerns nine (9) Hazelnut trees, dropping their fruit into the waters for the salmon to feed upon and obtain knowledge of everything in the world. In Greek mythology, Hermes, a messenger god was said to carry a staff made from a Hazel tree which aided his travels through the realms of both spirits and humans. Mercury (Roman mythology) is often depicted with a Hazel staff providing him with great wisdom. In our tale, Little Red Cap indicates further knowledge of this Wolf when she states, "… as you probably know," when she refers to the Hazelnut hedges and the three (3) large oak trees at her grandmother's house.

The **Oak Tree** is a symbol of strength, morale, resistance and knowledge. Throughout history, it is connected to powerful gods, as in Greek mythology it was a symbol of Zeus. In our tale, it is a masculine element of support for the richly feminine nature of the forest. That Little Red Cap's grandmother has the support of three (3) of these large trees is noteworthy, as we know of the need for the feminine, in order to have the balance provided by the masculine.

The **Grandmother/Mother/Daughter** trinity of the feminine, the sacred feminine, is an ancient symbol continually cycling through the three stages of womanhood. It's a powerful symbol of birth, growth, death and renewal. In addition, this trinity of the feminine gives rise to the numerology of the number three (3), which is the number assigned to the masculine. Therefore, contained within this feminine trinity is the recognition of the influence of the masculine. This awareness can be seen in the genetic representation of the female, with two XX's, contrasted by the male with one X and one Y, or XY. The X contains the Y within it. The Y is forever in search of completion. Psychologically, this completion is accomplished through the anima, the energy of the feminine, to be found within each man.

**Fl**owers symbolize springtime, happiness, wealth, abundance, fortune, prosperity, hospitality, joyfulness, beauty, and purity. In our tale, we are told of Little Red Cap's self-absorption when this wolf admonishes her, "…Look at the beautiful flowers growing about. Why don't you look around? I believe, you don't even hear the birds sweetly singing. You are walking absorbed in yourself…" The tale then progresses with Little Red Cap *opening her eyes* [she is no longer asleep] and seeing the sunlight in the woods, as if for the first time. Opening her eyes indicates a newly evolved aspect of her consciousness now available to her. In addition, she sees all the beautiful Flowers and, deciding to pick a bouquet for her grandmother, she quickly moves off the designated path, moving deeper and deeper into the woods (the unconscious).

The Flowers also bring in the recognition of Little Red Cap's return to a childhood innocence that was taken from her by being "crowned" too early in her life by her grandmother. Flowers are a great symbolic representation of The [Alchemical] Axiom of Maria Prophetissa, "One becomes two, two becomes three, and out of the third comes the one as the fourth:" The seed (1)—earth, planted in the ground; the *stem* (2)—air, movement toward the heavens, opposites of heaven and earth uniting; the *leaf* (3)—fire, via the process of photosyntheses, which requires the light from the sun; and the *blossom/flower* (4) returning to *seed* (1)—water, required for germination.

Her departure from the designated path shows an aspect of newly expressed rebellion in Little Red Cap, as she has found direction from within herself and not only from her mother. This departure not only gives **Wolf #1** more than ample time to get to grandmother's house—once there, he swallows up the grandmother, after which, he "puts her cloths on, puts on her bonnet, lays himself in her bed, and pulls the curtains to,"—but it also provides time to get into grandmother's bed.

The **Bed** is symbolically a place of vulnerability. As such in our tale, it reveals the cross-dressing/gender confusion dynamic of the adolescent Wolf #1. By pulling the curtains together, he conceals not only his cross-dressing gender confusion, but also the reality that he has gobbled up her grandmother. Little Red Cap, in her determination to find grandmother, pulls back the curtains, revealing both of Wolf #1's secrets. Having made such a discovery, she now finds herself in harm's way, and is gobbled-up.

By not assigning gender, Little Red Cap in our Fairy Tale's title, signifies both the potential for gender confusion and the alchemical opus of the hermaphrodite—the balanced, integrated, masculine and feminine. Psychologically, this is the ultimate result of individuation. Spiritually, it is the experience of an opportunity for co-creation. Writing this commentary and analysis in the 21st century provides more of a view from the portal of the *contrarian*. Historically, through the study of indigenous cultures, the contrarian title was assigned to those people who did not find solace in their birth gender assignment. This confusion often emerges in the pre-pubescence and early years of puberty when the biological hormones are in flux. Shamans are often identified by this trait of being able to represent both genders. Further evidence of how Wolf #1 is a shaman/healer/trickster follows later in this analysis.

The **Hunter** makes his appearance in our tale to save the grandmother and Little Red Cap. The Hunter archetype is one of an instinctual quest to know aspects of the self found in the rich environments of the unconscious. Therefore, he also carries a trinity of a bumbling/sacred/mean-spirited focus for his intensions. The significance of a Hunter in any story is in relationship to a quest, a hunting for something. In fact, the Hunter in our tale has been hunting for this Wolf, "...you old sinner...I have hunted you a long time." It was the sound of his snoring that alerted him that something might be wrong (sacred, with his sensitivity to potential danger) with the grandmother. As the Wolf was asleep, the Hunter was able to use the scissors (usurping the mean-spirited impulse to shoot him with his rifle) to cut him open, revealing not only the Grandmother but Little Red Cap as well. As the until-now-absent father (bumbling without conscious intention) almost as a *dumbling,* he appears at exactly the right time to save both Little Red Cap and her grandmother. [The dumbling in Fairy Tales is often the son of a king who, in spite of himself, gets the prize seemingly by accident.]

It is not a surprise to find a Hunter in the woods as the Forest is a place for hunting. In our tale, the three (3) Maiden/Mother/Grandmother have all been in search of masculine representations to balance with their feminine natures. As the father figure, the Hunter moves into action by cutting open the Wolf and releasing the Grandmother and Little Red Cap from the body of Wolf #1.

Scissors are a tool used for separating, opening/entry, in general, an ambiguous symbol, as they refer to cutting a life thread, and also represent the union of the spiritual and physical. In our tale, the Scissors function both to open the Wolf so the now transformed (having been gestated in the body of the Wolf, a masculine symbol) Grandmother and Little Red Cap emerge in another stage of consciousness. Also, the Scissors assist the Hunter in obtaining the pelt of the Wolf.

Stones are often used to symbolize the passage from one life to the next. They are believed to carry spirt energy as in Germany, the spirit of the dead remains in the tombstone, while many African beliefs hold to the idea that Stones carry the spirit of an ancestor. As a symbol of the divine, they mark the many struggles to overcome and perspectives to be gained. Many myths, fables, and stories use Stones as symbols of the obstacles characters must overcome to complete their quest. There is a mesmerizing quality that Stones have of taking on both cold and heat. In our tale, Stones were put inside the Wolf once the Grandmother and Little Red Cap were removed from his body. It can be said that he was weighed down with the spirits that were captured in the Stones. As his ability to overcome any further obstacles was now gone, he collapsed with the weight of those Stones and died.

**Velvet** has historically been a rich, expensive fabric made on special looms, most often from silk. The fabric is plain on the back, thick and soft on the front and, as such, it has symbolized power and wealth, not unlike Wolf #1's pelt. The Grandmother's use of Velvet fabric to make the cap for her Granddaughter indicates assignment of richness, power, and strength beyond the grasp of such a young maid. After his long pursuit of the "old sinner," the Hunter's booty of the Wolf's pelt provides the masculine with the appropriate assignment of richness, power, and strength.

The **Red Velvet Cap** she gives to her Granddaughter can be viewed as a crown, which forces Little Red Cap into precociousness, thereby usurping her childhood. Such an adornment set her apart from others her age, which is an example from alchemy of the "reddening coming too fast." Psychologically when childhood is interrupted by living out of a false persona of pseudo-maturity, it can alienate the child from others. This *painted-bird* phenomena, where others in the flock recognize the difference in the one painted, can cause severe alienation and even death as often the other birds will attack and kill the painted one. There is a time for the "reddening" to occur, a time that won't set the person on a collision course with the collective, as in this reference to the painted bird. Little Red Cap's velvet cap has set her on a potential collision course.

The **Resurrection** of both the maid and her Grandmother, when they come out of the body of Wolf #1, announces a new level of awareness for both of them. This new awareness (consciousness) is apparent in how they both deal in the encounter with Wolf #2. This new awareness can provide Little Red Cap with the energies she will need to "fit in" to her community, rather than stand dangerously alone and apart from them.

**Wolf #2** is a grey wolf, indicating that he is an older wolf. His encounter with Little Red Cap shows a maturing in how he relates to Little Red Cap and Grandmother with more patience than Wolf #1. In addition, the evolution in consciousness of both Little Red Cap and the Grandmother is validated by how they relate to the wolf with more maturity—Little Red Cap, by noting the look in his eyes that made her fearful and Grandmother, by using what was available and making a plan for Wolf #2's demise. She and her Grandmother are able to plot against the grey Wolf and provide safety for themselves by bringing about the death of this Wolf.

The **Sausages** are the bait used by Little Red Cap and her Grandmother in luring the grey Wolf to his death. Sausages and hot dogs carry the power of the meat and herbs out of which they are made, although Sausages of all types represent zestful, male energy (fire). The fiery male energy is now available to the Grandmother and Little Red Cap, an indication of integration of the masculine and feminine energies within each of them. In our tale, the cooking of the Sausages is another example of the maturation of the masculine—moving from the raw to the cooked.

The **Stone Trough,** remembering the symbolism of Stone, functions as a container for both spirit and water and, much like the glass Bottle, it also represents the alchemical vessel of containment for transformations facilitated by heat. In our tale, the heat of cooking the Sausages, as well as the heat of angry passion, allows this Stone trough to be the final resting place for Wolf #2.

**Water** is a primary component in cooking, as well as in most alchemical processes. Our tale explains how Grandmother had used Water in the cooking of the Sausages the day before Little Red Cap's visit, so it is now available for another use. When Water or tea is allowed to sit in the sun for 4-6 hours, it is considered psychically discharged or "balanced." Knowing this Water had been sitting for more than a day lets us know that it is psychically discharged and balanced, yet another indication of the new balance now within the Grandmother and Little Red Cap.

In this tale, the **Senses** of sight, touch, taste, hearing, and smell are each present. **Sight** is evident, when by opening her eyes, Little Red Cap perceives the Woods/Forest as if seeing it for the first time when Little Red Cap approaches her Grandmother's bed and sees the big ears, eyes, hands,

and mouth, of Wolf #1 and, later, when she sees the fear-producing look in the eyes of Wolf #2, the grey Wolf. **Touch**, is demonstrated when Little Red Cap is picking the Flowers, when Wolf #1 grabs both the Grandmother and Little Red Cap in order to gobble them up, when Little Red Cap fetches the Stones to put inside of the Wolf, and when the Hunter drew off the Wolf's pelt. **Taste** is indicated when the mother provides the Cake and Wine for Little Red Cap to take to the Grandmother and when Wolf #1 reflects on the tastiness of Little Red Cap in contrast to the flavor of the Grandmother. **Hearing** is exhibited when Little Red Cap hears the birds in the woods/forest, as if for the first time. Another example of Hearing occurs when the Hunter, Hearing the snoring, becomes concerned enough to investigate the wellbeing of the Grandmother. In addition to the numerous conversations heard throughout the tale ,it is the knocking on Grandmother's door that announces the presence of each of the Wolves. **Smell** is implied by the Flowers, Cake, and Wine but, most importantly, through the fragrance in the Water that cooked the Sausages.

In the beginning of our tale, there is an evolution—with the opening of Little Red Cap's eyes—that makes manifest all five senses. As our tale progresses, after the gestation in Wolf #1's body, a **Sixth Sense** becomes available to both the Grandmother and Little Red Cap. The Grandmother was able to intuit the intention of the Grey Wolf, and Little Red Cap was able to discern the bad/mean look in his eyes that caused her to be both cautious and fearful. Both of these are examples of the ability to trust and rely on **intuition**. Little Red Cap's trust was out of ignorance at the beginning of our tale in following the instructions of Wolf #1 to leave the path. By the end of our tale, trust *with* Intuition shows the benefit of the evolution of maturing consciousness in Little Red Cap.

# Depth Psychology Analysis

### Sacred Geometry

The most dominant figure from Sacred Geometry represented in this tale is that tetrahedron. The tetrahedron is the sacred geometrical figure for fire. As such, we see how fire has multiple expressions from the cooking of the cake and sausages to the emotional passion of love (the grandmother's love for her granddaughter) and the passionate anger needed to bring about the demise of Wolf #2.

### Numerology

**Number 1,** as the number for destiny, is evident first in our title, as Little Red Cap refers to a singular character. We then find, in our opening paragraph, a little girl who has been given a red cap by her grandmother, so we know the focus of the destiny journey will be hers.

The grandmother/mother/daughter trinity of the feminine, the hunter and the two wolves trinity of the masculine and the opposites of the masculine and the feminine represent the **Number 2**. The number 2 is a feminine number.

**Number 3** appears in the dual trinities of grandmother/mother/daughter and the hunter and the two wolves. The number 3 is a masculine number.

**Number 4** is recognized from the wholeness of the elements water, fire, air, and earth, reflecting the balanced environment in which our tale takes place. In our tale, there are various subtle references to the four elements of wholeness. Here are just a few: *air* is recognized from speech, snoring, and breath; *water*, from the sausage water that Wolf #2 drowns in; *earth*, from the cake and the woods/forest; and *fire*, from the emotion of obsessed passion the grandmother feels for her granddaughter, from the fire cooking the cake and the sausages, and from the passionate anger necessary to cause the demise of Wolf #2.

Numerological significance is given to the **Time** references in the second paragraph of our tale, when Little Red Cap is describing the distance in time from her village to grandmothers house: 15 minutes = 1+5 = 6, and 30 minutes = 3+0 = 3, bringing the number (6+3 = 9) assigned to this tale as the **Number 9**. The number 9 is indicative of the completion of a cycle. In addition, it is the number for those who accomplish the divine will and is also a symbol of wisdom and intuition. Remember, from the earlier mention of the Celtic myth, there were nine (9) Hazelnut trees surrounding the waters where the salmon would gain all wisdom from the nuts falling into the water.

## Colors

The dominant color for this tale is **Red**. Some of the associations for the color "red" are the root chakra, life force, anger, and passion. A colloquial expression often used, "waving a red flag in front of a bull," gives rise to the awareness of how an elegant cap of red sets apart our protagonist, Little Red Cap. The wine moved our color, red, toward a deeper dimension representing the necessary healing enchantments provided by the mother and needed by the grandmother.

At the direction of Wolf #1, Little Red Cap was instruct to "...look at the beautiful flowers growing about. Why don't you look around?" As we will see in the alchemical description that follows, Wolf #1 is catalytic in bringing a **Rainbow of Colors** worthy of Little Red Cap's awakening perceptions.

Of interest to me, is that Wolf #2 brings the color **Grey**. We know from its designated color that it is an older wolf. However, from a psychological interpretation of this dynamic found in the color grey in the tale, a forecast of the movement in consciousness for Little Red Cap and her grandmother exists by indicating the evolution from the black-and-white into a more multidimensional world view.

## Chakras

All chakras are evident, specifically, with Little Red Cap and her mother. The **7th Chakra** represents the connection with divine intelligence. We see this through mother's wisdom of knowing the needs, both of her mother, due to her illness and her daughter, due to her need to release aspects of her false maturity which set her apart from her peers. Intuition, represented by the **6th Chakra,** the crown chakra, appears in our tale when Little Red Cap responds to the glean in the eye of the Grey Wolf. The **5th Chakra,** representing communication, manifests most obviously when Little Red Cap uses her voice when she encounters Wolf #1 in bed wearing her grandmother's clothing. The heart chakra, the **4th,** is seen through the compassionate heart of Little Red Cap, by her demonstrated respect for both her mother and grandmother. Personal power, represented by the **3rd Chakra,** sometime known as the solar plexus, is central to our tale as Little Red Cap must become her own person and not continue to live out of a false persona. The **2nd Chakra** provides the energies for relationships. Our entire tale is about a variety of relationships. The **1st Chakra,** known as the root chakra, is the home of kundalini energy. It is often referred to as the center for tribal connections and, therefore, survival. This tale ultimately captures Little Red Cap's destiny through awareness of her life-force.

## The Alchemical Process

As we enter into the alchemical treatment of this Fairy Tale, we do so with the awkward knowledge of the "reddening coming too fast" for Little Red Cap. An alchemical adage warned practitioners of that art against the "reddening coming too fast." This is much like the warning from Eastern traditions, of kundalini rising too fast, which can cause, among other things, a psychotic episode in some individuals. From our opening paragraph, we enter into an awareness that our protagonist, Little Red Cap, by the action of her grandmother giving her the velvet cap (a crown), was at risk of this experience of pseudo-maturity (precociousness, even psychosis). The reader, now being cognizant of this adage, when reflecting upon the need for caution, understands how the lessons that are provided for our protagonist must occur. It was her mother's intuition and wisdom that put her on the divine journey of her destiny, circumventing further expression of her handicap (being crowned too soon).

This tale provides an impressive window into the alchemical process and, therefore, the individuation process in relationship to the integration of the masculine (animus) and the feminine (anima). As the feminine is represented through the maiden/mother/crone trinity, we have known from the very first paragraph that the pursuit of the masculine was a direction in our tale. We know from the alchemical text, *The Secret of the Golden Flower*, that the animus *originates in the eyes*. Wolf #1 assisted Little Red Cap in the experience of *opening her eyes*, which is an example of an aspect of her masculine (animus) energies becoming more available through her emerging consciousness. The wolf was so starved for his valid experience of the feminine (anima) that he literally put on the grandmother's clothing and lustfully gobbled up both the grandmother and Little Red Cap, taking them into his abdomen/body. Unmistakably, the hermaphroditic alchemical stage is seen here.

Little Red Cap's mother promotes a new beginning for Little Red Cap on the morning she instructs Little Red Cap to participate in her grandmother's healing and, thereby, sets out on a journey that will provide an opportunity for her to move away from living out of her precocious handicap. It is morning when her mother gives Little Red Cap this challenge. An hour is a representation of wholeness, so the time references that come up in that paragraph are about a fresh start, a new beginning.

Although, not yet consciously aware of the intricacies of her destiny's journey, Little Red Cap shares deep wisdom in relationship to the timing of this day's journey. This is known to us from her recognition of grandmother's house being 30 minutes into the woods from the village and when she encounters Wolf #1, she knows she has another 15 minutes to go.

*Nigredo* (black): This first stage provides for the recognition of shadow presences, archetypal and complex representations, as well as projections. The mother is the medial place holder between the sick grandmother and the "painted-bird handicap" of our protagonist, Little Red Cap. In her insistence that Little Red Cap get on her way before it gets too hot, the mother is showing her awareness that Little Red Cap will not evolve if she continues living out of the inflated space of being crowned too soon (Little Red Cap's handicap).

*Albedo* (white): This second stage provides opportunities for communications between the masculine (*animus)* and feminine (*anima)* aspects of the psyche. From our tale, it is known that both the feminine maiden/mother/crone and the masculine bumbling/mean-spirited/sacred hunter and two wolves are in search of relationship/dialogue with each other.

*Citrinitas* (yellow): This third alchemical stage recognizes the role of the journey. This requires finding relatedness with the outer world and experiencing issues of transference and countertransference, as both provide opportunities for developing evolving consciousness in relationship with the Self. Little Red Cap's ability to relate to the masculine is witnessed with the Wolf #1 in the woods/forest, and at grandmother's house, as well as with the Hunter, as she assists with the elimination of Wolf #1 by bringing the stones. Later recognition of a fear-producing spirit in Wolf #2 that she did not see in Wolf #1, along with her collaboration with her grandmother in bringing about the demise of Wolf #2, indicate her evolving consciousness.

*Rubedo* (red): This fourth alchemical stage honors the results of the first three processes. In our tale, the catalytic instructions from the mother brought about the destiny journey not only for Little Red Cap but, also, for the trinity of the feminine. From the quest, both for the masculine seeking the relationship with the feminine to the feminine in search of the masculine, the journey of destiny has occurred. Remembering the alchemical adage warning practitioners of alchemy against the "reddening coming too fast," it is now evident with the evolution of her consciousness that Little Red Cap has now **earned her crown**.

## Spirituality

The overall spiritual theme for this tale is that of **Resurrection**, as the Christian ritual of communion, representing the body and the blood, can be compared to the cake and wine being brought to the grandmother. In the Christian myth, Christ has the Disciples eating the bread and drinking the wine, with the knowledge that through his death, he would be born into another dimension (consciousness). Similarly, in our tale, the feminine is reborn into another level of consciousness. The re-birth of both Little Red Cap and her grandmother, as they are reborn out of the body of Wolf #1 by the Hunter's use of scissors, brings about a new awareness (evolution of consciousness). Both the wisdom and the innocence of the feminine archetype needed to be co-mingled in the body of the masculine, represented by Wolf #1, thereby allowing deep influence of the other and providing the opportunity to participate in **Co-creation**. Alchemically, Wolf #1 functioned as a vessel. This union of the opposites of wisdom and ignorance was necessary for an evolution of consciousness within the feminine. Once again, in our tale, the awareness of the opportunity for Co-creation with the Divine manifests through the evolution of consciousness. With the cycle completed (9), an aspect of the combined destinies of Little Red Cap, the mother, and the grandmother (maiden/mother/crone), has been fulfilled.

# CHAPTER 2

# 25

# The Seven Ravens

Translated from the original German version of the Grimms
Fairy Tale collection

# 25

# The Seven Ravens[16]

A man had seven sons and still no little daughter, as much as he wished for one. Finally, his wife again gave him high hope for a child, and when it came into the world, it was indeed a little girl. His happiness was great, but the child was small and thin, and because of its weakness, had to have an emergency baptism. The father sent one of the boys in haste to the well[17] to fetch baptismal water. The other six ran along, and because each [of them] wanted to be the first to draw water, the bucket fell into the well. There they stood and did not know what they should do, and none of them dared to go home. When they still did not return, the father became impatient and said, "Certainly, they have again forgot ten it over a game, the godless boys." He was afraid the little girl would have to die unbaptized, and in anger he cried, "I wish that the boys would all turn into ravens." Hardly had the words been uttered, then he heard a whirring in the air over his head, looked up, and saw seven coal-black ravens flying up and away.

---

[16] **The Seven Ravens** -- Die Sieben Raben, a direct translation.

[17] **well** -- *Quelle*, which carries primarily the connotation of "spring" or "source."

The parents could not take the enchantment back again, and as sad as they were over the loss of their seven sons, they comforted themselves somewhat with their dear little daughter, who soon recovered her strength and became more beautiful with each day. For a long time, she did not even know that she had had siblings,[18] for the parents were careful not to mention them, until one day by chance, she heard people talking about her, saying the girl was certainly beautiful, but still guilty of the misfortune of her seven brothers. She became very distressed, went to her father and mother and asked whether she had had brothers and what had become of them? Now her parents could no longer keep the secret quiet, said, however, that it was a dis aster from heaven and her birth had only been the innocent cause. Only the girl's conscience bothered her daily, and she believed she would have to save her siblings again. She had neither peace nor rest,[19] until she could secretly be on her way and travel into the wide world to discover her brothers somewhere and to free them, cost what it may. She took nothing with her other than a little ring from her parents as a memento, a loaf of bread for her hunger, a little pitcher of water for her thirst, and a little stool for her fatigue.

---

[18] **siblings** -- *Geschwister*, which is usually translated as "brother(s) and sister(s)." Other translations render this as "brothers."

[19] **peace nor rest** - nicht Ruhe und Rast, and idiom which means restless, but which conveys the emotions better if translated word for word.

She went on and on, far, far until the end of the world. Then she came to the sun, but it was too hot and terrifying and ate little children. Quickly, she ran away and ran to the moon, but it was entirely too cold and also horrible and evil, and when it noticed the child, it said, "I smell human flesh." Then she set off quickly and came to the stars, which were kindly and good to her, and each one sat on its special little chair. The morning star stood up, though, gave her a drumstick,[20] and said: "If you do not have the drumstick, you cannot unlock the glass mountain, and in the glass mountain are your brothers."

The girl took the drumstick, wrapped it carefully in a little cloth and walked farther, until she came to the glass mountain. The gate was locked, and she wanted to take out the drumstick, but when she opened the little cloth, it was empty, and she had lost the gift from the helpful[21] stars. What was she to do? She wanted to save her brothers and had no key to the glass mountain. Dear little sister took a knife and cut off one of her little fingers, stuck it in the gate, and fortunately unlocked it. When she had entered, a dwarf came toward her, who said,

---

[20] **drumstick** -- Hinkelbeinchen. I translate this as "drumstick" following the existing translations. Hinkel come from the verb hinken, "to limp," and Beinchen is the diminutive of Bein or "leg." Literally, what the morning star gives the girl is a "limping leg" or a "game leg." Add to the literal translation the fact that the devil in German folklore is often referred to as "Der Hinkende," "he who limps," the star's gift would seem to be some sense of mortality, of physical limitations, and of the "other" side, the world of the devil or, psychologically, of the unconscious.

[21] **helpful** -- The German here is gut, which means "good," of course. In this context, "well-meaning" or "helpful" seems more appropriate.

"My child, what do you seek?" -- "I seek my brothers, the seven ravens," she answered. The dwarf said, "The lord ravens are not at home, but come in, if you would like to wait until they return." Thereupon, the dwarf carried in the raven's food on seven little plates and in seven little tumblers,[22] and little sister ate a little piece from each little plate and from each little tumbler took a little sip. Into the last little tumbler, though, she let fall the little ring, which she had brought along.

6 **helpful** -- The German here is *gut,* which means "good," of course. In this context, "well-meaning" or "helpful" seems more appropriate.

7 **tumbler** -- *Becher.* I use "tumbler" here to make clear that the German is not *Tasse,* "cup."

Suddenly she heard a whirring and a blowing in the air, [and] the dwarf said, "Now the lord ravens come flying home." Then they arrived, wanted to eat and drink, and looked for their little plates and little tumblers. One after another, they said, "Who has eaten from my little plate? Who has drunk out of my little tumbler? It was the mouth of a human being." And when the seventh came to the bottom of his tumbler, the little ring rolled toward him. He looked at it and recognized that it was a ring from [his] father and mother and said, "God grant that our little sister were here. Thus we would be saved." When the girl, who stood behind the door and listened, heard his wish, she came

---

[22] **tumbler** -- Becher. I use "tumbler" here to make clear that the German is not Tasse, "cup."

out, and all the ravens regained their human form again. They embraced and kissed one another and went happily home.

*translated by Gary V. Hartman,*
*© 1997 Gary V. Hartman*

*Illustration by Anna Leamon*

## Artist's Comments

When I read a story with the intention of illustrating it, usually an image will present itself to me and that's where I begin the illustration process.

In the case of the Seven Ravens, three things stood out to me first. The anxiety the sister began to feel when she learned she was the cause of the brothers absence, the second was her long journey—which took her away from the familiar and into the magical, and the third thing would be the image of the seven ravens.

Inspired by old storybook illustrations that often use panels and borders and rich jewel tones, I attempted to capture main points of the story, as well as the mood of the tale to draw the readers deeper into their own imagination.

# #25

# The Seven Ravens
# Commentary and Analysis

Lois Wilkins, PhD, APRN

# Commentary

This commentary explores the characters found in the #25, "The Seven Ravens," The significance of each character provides a portal to explore the dynamic of timelessness, multidimensionality, and the depth psychological analysis that follows this commentary.

## Title

The language of numerology is immediately brought to the tale by the number Seven (7) in this title. Seven indicates completion and accomplishments well done. Ravens are birds that throughout history, in various myths and folklore, have often been presented as messengers from the gods between the worlds of life and death. Their messages can be either positive or ominous. From this title, we know the tale is focused on fulfillment and an array of messages.

## The Initial Paragraph

In the first paragraph, we learn of a **father** who, although he has **seven sons**, wishes that he had a daughter. His **wife** does finally gives birth to a **daughter**, but because the baby is small, weak, and sickly her parents believe she must have an emergency baptism. The father sends one of his sons to fetch the baptismal waters and the other six brothers run along with him. Disaster occurs when all the brothers, fighting over the bucket, cause it to fall into the well. The **boys**, knowing they have failed their sister and disappointed their parents, are afraid and do not dare to return home.

Awaiting their return, the impatient father fears the daughter will die and laments, "Certainly, they have again forgotten it over a game, the godless boys." In his fear and anger, he cries out, "I wish that the boys would all turn into ravens." His wish is granted. In fact, the Father has two (2) wishes granted in this first paragraph: one for good, to have a daughter; and one for ill, to turn his seven sons into **ravens**.

From the first paragraph, the movement of this tale involves magic/enchantment. The father is unaware of the power in his words. The movement is from the masculine toward the healthy feminine. Initially, we are introduced to a small, weak, sickly baby girl, alerting us that the feminine is going to have to show a large presence, gain strength, and become well. We also know that the emotions of anger, fear, and anxiety permeate this family system. We know this by the behavior of the father and his seven sons. Both the father and mother are anxious about the wellbeing of the newborn daughter and their ability to protect her.

## Main Characters

The **Parents**, having long wished for a daughter and finally, after seven sons, having their wish granted, demonstrate fear and anxiety. We will learn that these emotions of fear and anxiety have contaminated their sons. This is not uncommon, psychologically, for the emotional atmosphere in the home to play out in the children. Magical thinking is a defense mechanism used by the father when, out of his fear and anger, he wishes for his sons to be turned into ravens. The reality that the magical thinking results in a powerful enchantment leaves both parents regretful and sad. They are somewhat comforted by the attention they can bestow on their now healthy, beautiful daughter.

Not wanting to burden their daughter with the story of the misfortune of her seven brothers, the parents decide to keep them a secret and not even let her know she has seven brothers. The parents, when confronted by their daughter, learn that she overheard people talking about her seven brothers. They then confess, claiming their deception around a disaster from heaven, with the daughter's birth being an innocent cause.

The **Seven (7)** sons act as a collective unit and in being assigned to the fetching of the baptismal waters demonstrate a rather pagan irreverence to Christianity. Although the father sends one of the boys to get the baptismal waters from the well, the other six (6) boys run along with him. In their competitive play, they end up losing the bucket into the well; this failure to bring the baptismal waters to their baby sister causes them anxiety and fear over what they believe will be her certain death and damnation to hell (as she will not be baptized before her death). Immobilized by their collective fear and anxiety, they do not return home. When the boys did not return home, their father's fear, anger, and anxiety is compounded. In his tumult, the father utters an enchantment, wishing his sons to be turned into ravens, as he now believes they are godless. His wish is granted; they are turned into seven ravens and fly up and away.

**Ravens,** according to Greek mythology, are associated with Apollo, the god of prophecy and, as such, bring messages, both good and bad. They are seen as the messengers from the gods to earthly mortals. Raven symbolism, according to depth psychology, is a representation of the shadow aspects of the self that are unknown to consciousness. Also, they represent the bird of death and the afterworld. Woton, the pagan god, often referenced as Odin or a Sun God, had two ravens associated with him, Huginn and Mininn, representing thought and memory.

The ravens in our tale force the parents to see and begin the process of communicating with unknown parts of themselves. The boys, until they were turned into ravens, were acting as collective extensions of the father's desires. Once the father's anger, fears, and anxieties gave voice to seeing the godless aspects of his boys, the portal was opened for him to acknowledge his darker side. Raven symbolism promotes communication with both sides of ourselves. Unconsciously, the father was calling on the energy of the ravens to promote communication between the light and dark sides of himself. In other words, from the consistent unveiling of inner depth, the positive impulses of bringing light into the darkness were made manifest.

The **Daughter** entered this family system, after her seven brothers, as small, thin, and weak. Her frailty frightened the family, so much so, that it was believed she would not survive for long and, therefore, was in need of an emergency baptism. This tells us that she was born into a God-fearing family.

As she grows in health and beauty, her parents are careful to never make mention of her brothers. In overhearing the townspeople talking about her, she learns that they think she must feel guilty over the misfortune of her seven brothers. With this information, she becomes distressed and confronts her parents. Although her parents can no longer keep the secret of her brothers from her, they do frame the incident as "...a disaster from heaven and that her birth had only been the innocent cause."

As her guilt bothers her daily, she grows to believe she will have to save her brothers again. Her first act of saving her brothers is to reclaim them into the family system by forcing her parents to speak of their existence. To save them for a second time, she must find a way to release them from the curse and bring them back into the family system. Therefore, she decides to secretly be on her way to find her brothers and set them free of the enchantment—at all costs.

For her journey, she takes four items, "…a little ring from her parents as a memento of them, a loaf of bread for her hunger, a pitcher of water for her thirst, and a little stool for her fatigue." On her journey to the end of the world, she encounters the hostile sun and moon and the helpful stars, the most helpful being the morning star, which gives her instructions on how and where she can find her brothers. Having established destiny's path with the assistance of the morning star, she continues on her journey to reclaim her brothers.

## Characters and Symbolism of Images

In our tale, the **Sun** represents the archetypal negative energy found in her father. Living out of ignorance, as he is unaware of his dual nature, he unknowingly and without consciousness brings about the enchanted curse that changes the boys into ravens. Not surprisingly, after reaching the end of the earth, our heroine approaches the Sun, discovering it is "too hot and terrifying and ate little children." Discovering the Sun as the negative archetypal father in his punitive, frightening, and angry behaviors, she experiences greater fear and anxiety.

Likewise, the **Moon** represents the archetypal negative energy found in her mother. Her mother's ignorance of her own dual nature is expressed by her cold, non-engaging relationship with her daughter. Potentially, a fused relationship is represented here, as there is no separateness from the mother's desires and what she projects onto her daughter. Psychologically, we know this dynamic of relationship fusion forces the daughter to carry out her journey in *secret*. This secrecy is necessary in order for the daughter to begin her journey of individuation. By withholding defining aspects of her daughter's life from her, unable to mirror healthy separation between the mother and daughter, the townspeople (collective) bring awareness of those unknown aspects of life to the daughter. The Moon mirrored this negative archetypal mothering dynamic by being "entirely too cold and also horrible and evil, and when it noticed the child, it said, 'I smell human flesh.'" Here, in the desire to eat the daughter, is an example of the devouring mother, unable to separate from her daughter.

The **Stars and their Little Chairs** provide new potential for our heroine on her secret journey. Our heroine has had to travel to the ends of the earth, to the Sun and the Moon, before she can find the positive mirroring provided by the Stars sitting on their little chairs. The Stars have their little chairs, like the heroine has her stool. Too long, this relationship with positive mirroring has been out of our heroine's reach. Now, on her secret journey, her soul's journey, *a journey only she can take*, the positive mirroring happens. Often, in depth psychology, individuals are referred to as a "universe unto themselves," as are the universes assigned to each Star. The Stars and their little chairs provide new self-reflections that, until now, have been out of the reach of our heroine.

Venus is a planet and, as such, a representative of feminine energy. Commonly, Venus is referred to as the Morning Star because of its brightness. The (**Dwarf**) **Morning Star,** a planet, is a powerful catalyst for the success of our heroine's journey. Later, under "Symbolism," we will learn the significance of my assignment of a "Dwarf" to the Morning Star in our tale. With the morning star, we have an encounter with the *positive* archetypal feminine, as it provides our heroine with direction and instruction, while giving her the entrance key to the glass mountain that holds her brothers. The key, in the form of the drumstick, will allow for her entrance into the glass mountain.

The **Dwarf** guards the entrance to the glass mountain, and he provides for the wellbeing of the ravens. He does this by acting as their host and caretaker in this realm of base, instinctual, non-human existence of the brothers—as ravens.

A **Wish** is distinguished from a prayer in this manner. A prayer can be experienced as a collapse of personal power toward an external benefactor. Furthermore, prayer is a reach toward an energy outside most individuals, releasing the outcome to an external entity. On the other hand, a Wish is generated from within the individual's egocentric (personal) desires that will make manifest deeply personal outcomes. *Wishful thinking* is a defense mechanism, overriding logical conclusions. In our tale, the belief that their daughter would never learn of her brothers' existence gives us an example of the parents' wishful thinking.

There are three wishes granted. The first is from the father to have a daughter. The second is that the boys would become ravens and, as such, due to the unconscious nature of this wish, became a curse and an enchantment that could not be undone. The third wish is granted when the seventh brother proclaims, "God grant that our little sister were here. Thus we would be saved." With their sister's emergence from behind the door, all seven ravens regain their human forms, now as men.

When a personal desire (Wish) finds the wisdom of the importance of reigning in the external benefactor (Creator), the opportunity for living out of co-creation manifests. This is further explored in the Analysis under the section on spirituality.

Although a **Curse** is a deliberate, conscious action of a spell, psychologically, a projection can act on a person much like a spell. An example of a curse would be the pricking of Snow White's finger. It was a deliberate curse; it had a specific intention—to put Snow White to sleep. The curse had a deliberate, predetermined outcome. A conscious curse can be overturned when specific criteria are mastered, as in "Snow White," when she is kissed by the prince who was unaware that his kiss would reverse the curse.

An **Enchantment** is more of a buffoonery, as in our tale, where the father, in his unconscious lamentations, enchants his sons into becoming ravens. An enchantment, according to our tale, is overcome by the conscious intention of our heroine to overturn it and reclaim her brothers into the family.

Psychologically, the significance of **Secrets** in all Fairy Tales is that they exist in the realm of the unconscious. There are three examples of Secrets, in our tale, originating in the parents and in the daughter. Secrets become exposed by the light of consciousness. When the father is forced to acknowledge his buffoonery (unconscious intentions), causing the enchantment of his sons by turning them into ravens, our first secret is revealed. The main desire shared between the parents was to keep the existence of the brothers from their daughter. Both parents, now aware that they cannot reverse the enchantment, must begin the process of recognizing hidden, secret desires lurking within them. Their desire, in this second secret, was to protect their daughter and also themselves from guilt which the parents and the townspeople projected onto the daughter. The third secret is exposed when the daughter sets out on her *Secret* journey to reclaim her brothers and return them to the family system.

In her illustration, Anna Leamon depicts the cloaked sister on the path to the glass mountain. This silhouette of the dark, cloaked figure mimics the seven ravens in her illustration, emphasizing the veil of secrecy claimed by the daughter/little sister. The daughter/little sister's need to be secret about her journey demonstrates the psychological need to bring forth, from the unconscious, attributes to the family system. Once in the realm of consciousness, these heretofore secrets manifest the ability of the family to consciously evolve and be reunited.

The **Emergency Baptism** alerts the astute reader to the urgency this family feels in relationship to protecting the newly found feminine—the birth of the daughter. Unconsciously, the father recognizes his helpless and hopeless influence over the wellbeing of the feminine, which he perceives as small, thin, and weak.

From depth psychology and alchemy, we know that the masculine is in constant pursuit to find relationship with the feminine. This long-held desire of the father in our tale amplifies this psychological truth. It is not without precedence for the masculine, when confronted with the feminine, to perceive it as "small, thin, and weak." The fact that our heroine, the daughter/little sister, does not die without receiving the baptismal waters and, in fact, grows each day in beauty and strength, indicates how unaware the family is about the stronger aspects of the feminine. These aspects of the feminine are contrasted with the mother in this way: The mother, perhaps due to her overabundance of masculine demands, in caring for her husband and seven sons, has limited ability to be in touch with her own desires and only primitive influences cleaning and feeding for her husband and sons. On the other hand, the demands on the daughter remain closer to the divine, as we see by her ability to go on her secret journey. Her destiny is unknown to her until the revelation that she has seven brothers.

The father's lament for a daughter emphasizes the psychological need for him to have a more in-depth relationship with the feminine. What is initially perceived as small, thin, and weak, carries the projections of fears related to inadequacies of nurturing the evolving feminine.

**The Bucket** from our tale is at first, a symbol of hope for the containment of the baptismal waters. Due to the collective mass behavior of the seven sons, its function as a container is lost, no longer available. Psychologically, when containment is lost or broken, the transformational process is thwarted. In alchemy, the container has the capacity to either promote or retard transformation. In our tale, the townspeople contain the sons by holding them in awareness and by bringing awareness of their existence to the little sister. This containment is held until the little sister is ready to begin her and, ultimately, the brothers' transformation journeys—their destinies.

The **Ring**—a symbol of infinity, wholeness, and destiny—finds it way into our tale by the daughter's choice to take it from her parents as a reminder of them for herself and her brothers. The destiny of the family system is in the hands of the daughter as she goes on her secret journey. When the last brother, the seventh (7th) brother, drinks from his little tumbler, the ring, which little sister has dropped into it—rolls toward him. He recognizes this ring as one belonging to his parents, and exclaims: "God grant that our little sister were here. Thus we would be saved." The destiny of reuniting the family is about to be fulfilled.

The **Bread** taken on the journey by the sister indicates both her need to have sustenance and to provide nurturance for herself and the family as a whole. In other words, she is not naive about what can sustain and promote growth in her family, symbolically, not unlike the bread of life Christ provided for his followers.

Additionally, the **Water in the Pitcher** shows a functioning container that will not only quench her thirst on her journey, but also, psychologically resurrects the dynamic of containment for transformation that was lost with the bucket in the well. Water, as one of the basic elements for life, is further explored under the following analysis section on the alchemical processes.

In our tale, not only our heroine, but also, the stars all find benefit by resting—the stars on their chairs and our heroine on her **Stool**. After the encounters with the negative Sun and Moon, she discovers positive mirroring from the Stars. She is aware of this by seeing each of the stars sitting on their own special chair. For her, this reflects her own stool and, as such, she begins a relationship with positive mirroring.

**The Glass Mountain** is the place where the seven ravens, her brothers, live. The Morning Star tells our heroine how to get to the Glass Mountain in order to retrieve her brothers and gives her a gift of the key for entrance. Glass, in and of itself, is a paradox. It can be both strong when intact and useless when shattered. Glass, as an element, can be symbolic of the fragility of life issues. As such, fragile life issues can bring about redeeming strength or, if shattered, can bring about deadly shards.

The gift of the key, the **Drumstick,** from the Morning Star provides the method for entering the glass mountain. According to Hartman's footnote 5, he translates the drumstick with its literal meaning of a "limping leg" or a "game leg." Hartman tells us: "The fact that the devil in German folklore is often referred to as *'Der Hinkende,'* 'he who limps,' the star's gift would seem to be some sense of mortality, of physical limitations, and of the 'other' side, the world of the devil, or psychologically, of the unconscious."

This Drumstick is the gift from the Morning Star, representing the ability of the sister to carry the energies of the devil in harmony with herself. Yet, along the journey, she loses this devil's totem, so she cuts off one of her fingers to use it as a key. She is able to do this because she can now replace the external energy from the devil (Drumstick) with that of her own integrated energies of light and dark. Much like the red shoes worn by Dorothy in "The Wizard of Oz," our heroine was always in possession of the key for entrance into the Glass Mountain.

The **Key** in our tale is not only for opening the entrance to the Glass Mountain, but is also the entrance into the little sister's integration of light and dark aspects of herself. Having lost the key given by the Morning Star, the sister must now confront her insecurities (anxiety and fear). In so doing, she discovers her strength and ability to use the only resources available—her physical body (**Finger**) and a **Knife**.

The **Knife** used by the little sister to cut off one of her little fingers is an example from horror tales of fin-gore. This fin-gore is the deliberate use of a part of her body (**Finger**) as a replacement key, and as such, is a movement of consciousness beyond the realm of the physical body. This conscious separation moves her from the experiences of victimization and impotence caused by her fears and anxieties. Now, relying only on herself, the success of finding and reclaiming her brothers is within her reach.

In our tale the **Dwarf** manifests in two ways, one being a Dwarf star and, the other, the Dwarf character at the entrance to the Glass Mountain. In Germanic folklore, a dwarf is any member of a race of "little people" possessing specific supernatural powers. They are skilled and, therefore, often depicted as miners or metalworkers. The Dwarf at the entrance to the Glass Mountain symbolically provides awareness of the gestation required for the boys/ravens' evolution to men. Psychologically, the phase of adolescence involves a separation from childhood prior to the adult stage. Our boys/ravens, now having gestated in the womb of the Glass Mountain, have been prepared for their return to the family as men. Just as the Dwarf Morning Star facilitated the integration of light and dark with the sister, so has the Dwarf steward of the Glass Mountain facilitated the integrating dynamics of the boys/ravens to men.

Evidence that each of the seven (7) brothers has been nurtured while contained in the Glass Mountain is represented by **Seven Little Plates of Food and Seven Little Tumblers of Water.** Their little sister, partaking from each Little Plate and each Little Tumbler, indicates the influence of the feminine with each one of them. Once this uniting of the feminine with the masculine occurs, we again hear the whirling and blowing air, first experienced by the father the moment the boys were turned into ravens.

# Depth Psychology Analysis

In depth psychology, the never-ending quest toward more and more consciousness provides relevance for the study of Fairy Tales. Fairy tales, once analyzed psychologically, offer portals for moving the unconscious into consciousness. The identification of projections (unconscious) is a technique required in the analysis of Fairy Tales, which promotes opportunities to move such projections into awareness (consciousness). In our tale, secrets are just one example of this movement from the unconscious toward consciousness.

## Sacred Geometry

There is not a single geometric figure that influences this tale. This is because all five—the **tetrahedron** (fire), the **cube** (earth), **octahedron** (air), **dodecahedron** (spirit), **icosahedron** (water)— are easily recognized throughout the tale. Yet, for the purpose of this analysis, the most significant, when thinking of the enchantment which propelled the action of the tale is that of air, or the octahedron. This is because enchantment resides in the realm of subtle energies. In addition, the spirit, or dodecahedron, also has significance with the fulfillment of the destinies of the entire family in this tale.

Not to overlook how the other three sacred geometry figures play into the tale, let us recognize here the following roles. The fires of passion (tetrahedron) found within the desires of 1. the mother and the father to have a daughter; 2. the brothers to assist in their baby sister's emergency baptism; 3. the community to bring out of darkness the reality of the seven brother to the sister; and 4. the sister to return the brothers to the family.

In addition, earth (cube) is present as the family exists on earth and the baby girl being born, therefore, coming to earth. Also, we see the role of the waters (icosahedron) required for the baby girl's emergency baptism which sets the entire tale into motion, along with her awareness of the need for water to bring on her journey.

## Numerology

In numerology, the Number 7 can refer to completeness which manifests through holistic perfection. Our tale, "The Seven Ravens," supports the holistic perfection as it occurs through the multidimensionality of both light and dark attributes. In our tale, the Number 7 supports various combinations of numbers that equal seven (7) and finds a place between the two worlds, the world of life and the world of death, which the symbolism of ravens represents. As such, the evolution of human consciousness is forever promoting stages of completeness— those stages where rest occurs and those whose motion promotes the continuation of growth by the awareness of the need for regeneration. In our tale, the little sister has several years rest prior to learning of the existence of her brothers. Completion and regeneration are part of a never-ending cycle, the enantiodromia, the number 8, as the destinies of the little sister and her brothers demonstrate this continuous cycle. Likewise, in depth psychology, there is never a complete, stagnant integration of the masculine and feminine—unlike alchemy, where a final opus can manifest.

It is said that God rested on the 7th day, further supporting the number seven (7) numerology in a cycle of completion and holistic perfection. In our tale,"The Seven Ravens," completion is shown through numerology in the following examples. Keeping in mind that 2, 6, and 8 are assigned the energies of the feminine and 3, 5, 7, and 9 are relegated to the energies of the masculine, the following explanation provided. Knowing that three (3) is a masculine number and four (4), in addition to being a feminine number, is a quaternary number for wholeness, (3+4=7), we have a hint that there is, in the language of numerology, a message of the masculine in search of the wholeness that will be brought about by the feminine.

This is again emphasized with the number two (2), the union of the parents, representing the feminine energies of procreation, and the number five (5), being a numerological representative of the family (2+5=7). With the numerological language of the one (1) representing destiny and the six (6) representing the doubling of the three, which is an emphasis on the masculine, the seven ravens, (1+3+3=7). With 1+2+2+2=7, destiny (1), the mother (2), the little sister (2), and the parents' union (2), show us the energies of the feminine are also available as we move into the awareness of the destiny journey for the seven ravens and, therefore, the entire family.

Some say the language of numbers, numerology, is the basic code of the universe and as such provides this coded language for unpacking the depth meanings for growth and transformation explored through the characters in this tale. Our tale shows destiny's completion with 7+1=8, as the seven (7) ravens/men, with the one (1) little sister, brings together a wholeness that would not exist until they were reunited with a new level of consciousness.

## Colors

Although the reader can project many colors into this Fairy Tale, the tale itself only references the color of the ravens as "coal-black." This is very significant when reading the tale psychologically. Individuals, beginning their destiny journey at a level of primitive consciousness, begin the process of evolving consciousness by bringing awareness to facets of the self, often analogized as a diamond. With this simple descriptive term of the color coal-black, we are alerted to the primitive level of consciousness working within this family system. The father unconsciously projects aspects/facets of his dark unconscious onto his sons, due to the need of his soul's journey to advance the process of conscious evolution. In other words, there is no such thing as an accident.

The symbolism of the color black is that it holds, within it, all the other colors. Psychologically, the luminescence of the wings of the ravens—that oily, dark multi-color radiance—highlights the multiplicity of the separation dynamics out from the collective. This process of discernment is required for individuation to progress.

## Chakras

All seven chakras are evident in our tale, yet, although presented here in a linear fashion, they occur simultaneously as do all chemical processes.

> The **1st Chakra (Root)**, is most connected to the life-force energies concerned with survival. This chakra energy emerges in our tale with the father and mother's fears and anxieties over whether or not their baby girl can survive. This fear and subsequent anxiety manifest in sending the boys out for the emergency baptismal waters, showing us how deep they fear that she won't survive or be allowed into heaven if she is not baptized.

The **2nd Chakra (Sexuality/Procreation)** is demonstrated through the relationship that emerged among the family members: the relationship between the parents being about the desire for a daughter; the daughter's relationship to the family in her journey to return the brothers' to the family unit and; the collective relationship found with the brothers, first in their need to honor their fears of returning home after losing the baptismal waters and, ultimately, their collective desire to return home with their little sister as men.

The **3rd Chakra (Solar Plexus),** representative of personal/individual power, is demonstrated not only through the strength of the little sister as she grows out of her sickly introduction to the world. But, also, the personal power of the father as he is challenged in his ability to care for the feminine. This core insecurity is projected onto his sons, thereby contaminating their personal power, resulting in their fear of returning home after losing the bucket in the well.

The **4th Chakra (Heart)** was demonstrated by the passion in manifesting a daughter, the community bringing out of darkness the reality of the brothers, the compassion felt by the daughter, propelling her to begin her journey to bring wholeness to the family system by pursuing and returning her brothers.

The **5th Chakra (Throat)** is recognized through a variety of communications: the communication of the parents that they wanted a daughter; the communication of fears and anxieties among the brothers causing them not to return home; the father's buffoonery by communicating an unconscious desire, resulting in producing an enchantment that turned the seven sons into ravens; and the daughter's receiving the communications from the community, bringing to her awareness that, in fact, she had seven brothers.

The **6th Chakra (Intuition)** is shown in how the spell/enchantment produced turning the sons into ravens through the father's unconscious wishing. Also, intuition is revealed in the daughter's knowing that she could pursue the brothers and return them to the family.

The **7th Chakra (Divine Connection)** is evident in the destiny of the entire family to now live out of wholeness as they have evolved in their consciousness.

## The Alchemical Process

From our title, we are placed on alert that this entire tale could be seen to take place in the alchemical stage of *nigredo*. In the tale, we do not have a king and queen, we have a Father and a Mother and a Sun and Moon to represent both sides of parental archetypal influence. The difficulty in teasing out the alchemical process in a linear manner is that all processes happen simultaneously. Although our tale is grounded in the *nigredo* (the blackness, the beginning phase of alchemy), we can also see the destiny journey put into motion by the father's unconscious and the little sister's quest and success to return her brothers and bring the family to a new level of evolved wholeness/consciousness.

The father, as we have said, unconsciously put into motion the boys' adolescence which then occurs for each of them within a raven. By giving voice to his dark side, when he projects his frustrations, fury, and anxieties of being unable to care for the newly arrived daughter, he propels the boys into their own encounter with the dark side—a necessary part of adolescence. This projection of his unconscious desire to recognize the darkness within him acts as a spell on the boys, demonstrated by the enchantment which turns them into ravens. Psychologically, a projection can act as a spell for those on the receiving end until there is enough psychological awareness to reject such projections. The boys were ripe for receiving the father's projection/spell because of their own fear of returning home. They were also ripe to receive the father's projection because of their primitive psychological stage of living out of their collective, rather than having any awareness of the separation necessary for individuation. This struggle for the emergence of individuality is a hallmark of adolescence—when the group mind can have more influence than an individual's thoughts. Psychologically, this dynamic of living out of the collective is a necessary stage constellated in adolescence for the purpose of separating from the parents.

Upon receiving the enchantment from their father, the boys/ravens/men could then begin the processes of moving through the three stages. These three stages provide the recognition of the maturing of masculine attributes. By moving through the process of her destiny's journey, the little sister evolves from her small, thin, weak introduction to the family system and emerges as an empowered, strong, healthy younger sister.

Alchemically, the father's wish for a daughter brought forward the *family's destiny*, not unlike when Eve took the bite from the apple, which propelled human destiny. In alchemy, the element of **earth**, which is the One **(1)** from the Maria Prophetissa's axiom, "One becomes two, two becomes three, and out of the third comes the one as the fourth." The Two **(2)** in alchemy from this axiom is the *separatcio*, the separation of heaven and earth. The boys leave earthly bodies and take on the spiritual (**air**) bodies as ravens and fly between the two worlds. The Three (3) is paradoxically manifest in the little sister when she follows the energy of the masculine (*animus*) within her and sets out on her journey. *Animus* energy, representing the masculine is the Three **(3)** in the axiom and, as such the element of **fire**. The four (4) occurs within the ravens as they return to their human bodies, now as men; the little sister finds what always has been within her, the strength to enter into the glass mountain; and the family system is brought to completion with the return not only of the brothers, but also the little sister. Here, in the four (4), is the element of **water** which promotes the return to the one (1), now the *evolved family system*. The fluidity of human, family, and consciousness evolution is not unlike the memory in water, promoting life—all life has its origins in water.

## Spirituality

Some have said that the central theme of this tale is to "be careful what you wish for." This tale shows us the paradox of that saying. Without the capacity to wish, no one's destiny would be fulfilled. The father would have stayed in his ignorance of his dark side; the brothers would not have had the necessary separation from the family system that allowed their successful transition throughout adolescence, allowing them to return home as men; and in fact, the little sister would not have come into existence.

The emotions of anger, fear, and anxiety were absolutely critical for the father, his sons, and the little sister to experience. Had the father lived an idyllic life, he would have been like Job, before God brought all the pestilence and strife or like Adam and Eve, never leaving the ignorance of the perceived perfection of Eden, and numerous other examples of innocent/ignorant stagnation. Light and dark must be experienced by the individual in order for co-creation to occur. In other words, the divine would not find its way into human consciousness without the transformations possible because of the tension of opposites. In our tale, the parents were unaware

104

that there was anything other than what they were living out of and, therefore, they were not aware of opposites. It took the messaging from lived experiences, brought into awareness by their eight children, to bring the necessary changes of consciousness and the evolution toward the ultimate experience of co-creation.

This tale did not occur in the realm of a king and queen; it occurred in the realm of ordinary human beings. The messages found in this tale started in the space of the ominous, because there was such a primitive level of consciousness available to the parents. This is not unlike humanity's struggle to grow in the awareness of the Creator and the reality of not only humanity's own dark side, but also the emptiness/darkness within the Creator. Until an individual owns their own dark side, there is little opportunity to accept that the Creator could also have such a struggle.

We know from our title that the number seven (7) is going to show the dynamics of completion. This Fairy Tale provides an experience of a family system completing the tasks of maturation required for movement beyond a primitive level of consciousness. In this process, the reader can see the significance of a single family unit moving humanity forward toward co-creation.

# CHAPTER 3

# 23

# Concerning the Little Mouse, the Little Bird, and the Bratwurst

Translated from the original German version of the Grimms Fairy Tale collection.

# 23

# Concerning the Little Mouse, the Little Bird, and the Bratwurst[23]

Once a little mouse, a little bird, and a bratwurst fell into each other's company, maintained a household, and lived delightfully and well in peace and increased their holdings most admirably. The little bird's work was to fly into the forest daily and fetch wood. The mouse was supposed to carry water, light the fire, and set the table. The bratwurst was supposed to cook.

Whoever has it too good, always longs for new things! One day, therefore, the little bird came upon another bird along the way, to whom he described and praised his excellent circumstances. This same other bird called him a simpleton, all that work and the two at home have it easy.[24] For, when the mouse had lit the fire and carried water, she betook herself to her little chamber to rest until she was called on to set the table.

---

[23] Von dem Maüschen, Vögelchen und der Bratwurst. This is a literal translation. A Bratwurst is one of the most common German sausages, light casing and light filling, and is generally grilled. Hence the name, Brat from braten, to roast or grill, and wurst, sausage.

[24] **have it easy** -- gute Tage hätten, literally, "had good days."

The little sausage stayed by the pot,[25] saw to it that the food cooked properly, and when it was almost time to eat, coiled itself four times through the soup or vegetables and thus they were flavored, salted, and ready. When the little bird got home and lay down his burden, they sat down at the table, and after a completed meal, they slept to their hearts' content[26] until the next morning. And it was a wonderful life.

The next day, having been provoked, the little bird no longer wanted to go into the woods, saying he had been their servant[27] long enough and had to be their fool at the same time, they should trade places for a change and try it another way. And no matter how hard the mouse and the bratwurst, too, pleaded with him, the bird was master: it had to be chanced, they had to gamble for it, and the lot fell to the bratwurst, who had to carry wood, the mouse became the cook, and the bird was supposed to fetch water.

What happened? The little bratwurst went out toward the wood, the little bird lit the fire, the mouse put on the kettle and waited alone until the little bratwurst came home and brought wood for the next day. The little sausage remained so long on the

---

[25] **stayed by the pot** -- blieb beim Hafen, a literal translation. Hafen also means "port," so the play on words would be "stayed in port," contrasting the bratwurst's easy task with the bird's having to leave the house and go out into the woods.

[26] **their heart's content** - sich die Haut vol/. The literal meaning is, "their skin full."

[27] **servant** - Knecht, farm-hand, servant, laborer, a lower, menial position.

way, however, that both of them suspected that no good would come of it, and the little bird flew a ways in the air to meet him. Not far away it found a dog on the road who had chanced upon the poor bratwurst as free booty, grabbed it, and swallowed it down. The little bird accused the dog roundly of highway robbery, but words did not good for, claimed the dog, he had found false papers on the bratwurst, and because of them, he had to forfeit his life.

Sadly, the little bird took up the wood, flew home, and described what it had seen and heard. They were very despondent, but agreed to do their best and to stay together. Therefore, the little bird set the table, and the mouse prepared the food and wanted to dish it up and, like the little sausage before her, to coil and slide through the vegetables in the pot to flavor them. But before she got to the middle, she could go no farther and lost hair, skin,[28] and, thereby, her life.

When the little bird came and wanted to put the food on the table, there was no cook about. Distressed, the little bird threw the wood here and there, called and searched, but could not find his cook. Out of carelessness, the wood landed in the fire so that a blaze[29] arose. The little bird hurried to fetch water, the

---

[28] Hair, skin – The German reads, Haut und Haar, "skin and hair," which is an idiom meaning "completely." A "correct" translation would read, "and, thereby, completely lost her life." Rendering the idiom literally is more descriptive and graphic.

[29] Brunst, which means more heat, figuratively, and, literally, sexual desire or passion.

bucket slipped from his hands into the well and he with it, so that he could no longer recover, and could only drown.

translated by Gary V Hartman
© 1997 Gary V Hartman

*Illustration by Cindy Hutchison*

## Artist's Comments

I was in college when I became obsessed with stories from the Grimm brothers' collection of Fairy Tales. One of the tales, known to me at that time was called, "The Mouse, the Bird and the Sausage." I had more or less memorized the tale and told it to many of my friends. Each time that I would tell the tale, I would embellish and change it somewhat to make a connection with the listeners. One thing that remained the same with each narration was what I had envisioned as the point or moral of the tale.

I worked one summer as a girl scout counselor at a camp while I was still in college. I told the tale to my adolescent scouts. I tamed the tale down slightly for them, giving it a much happier ending, but still sticking to the original moral or purpose, as I perceived it to be.

The tale never left me, in the many decades since. When I was a substitute teacher, as a reward for their good behavior, I would tell the students the tale, again and again. I altered it, depending on the age group. I always, always enjoyed telling the tale. I would ask each class what they felt the point of the tale was. They always got it, at least as I had envisioned it.

The characters in the tale had met and had decided to form a home partnership, based on their own natural skills and strengths. The characters, the bird, the mouse, and the sausage lived in bliss for a while. But matters changed, as they often do, and regretfully, the duties of each character had changed as well. Needless to say, things did not end well.

I felt that the moral, meaning, point, whatever—was about envy, jealousy, and simply, that the characters felt their tasks were underrated; they were cheated and disrespected. Although the special skills that had originally formed the alliance had been successful, they wanted what they had perceived the others had—an easier life.

As some of my students would have said, "Be happy with what you have, and use your skills wisely."

# #23

# Concerning the Little Mouse, the Little Bird, and the Bratwurst Commentary and Analysis

Lois Wilkins, PhD, APRN

# Commentary

This commentary reflects on the unlikely alliance of a mouse, a bird, and a sausage. The tale recognizes a phase of the process of individuation known as circumambulation, which is the circling or movement around dynamics of individuation. The alchemical vibrational sciences are explored through specific representations of spirit, earth, air, water and fire found throughout the tale.

## Title

Immediately, this title, "Concerning the Little Mouse, the Little Bird, and the Bratwurst," recognizes a relationship exists between these three dissimilar characters. In addition, we know that the word "little," of course, refers to size but also can refer to innocence and youth. Beyond this, we also know with the use of the word "concerning" that perhaps something troublesome will arise or has arisen within their relationship. We also note from the title the lack of innocence with the Bratwurst: he is not referred to as "Little". By including the word "Concerning" in Hartman's translation, these subtleties are allowed to come through,—the subtleties of innocence and trouble.

## The Initial Paragraph

We meet our threesome aware from the first sentence with the use of the phase, "fell into each other's company," that there was a lack of conscious intention in their union. We can say they have come together unconsciously. Yet, in such a seemingly haphazard beginning, they have been able to maintain a household, delegate duties according to individual skill sets, and live in peace and prosperity, as noted by the increase "in their holdings most admirably."

Our Fairy Tale opens with an imbalance that alerts us to the need for the role to move toward a fourth character. This imbalance is shown in the fact that there are only three main characters. We know that the fourth must come from the feminine in order for wholeness to occur, since we have a masculine bird and a masculine bratwurst, with a feminine mouse.

The structure of wholeness, recognized as four-foldedness, is not present in the opening paragraph. For the careful reader, aware or in pursuit of the psychology and universal significance in Fairy Tales, there is evidence of the need for consciousness to be increased. Therefore, alchemically and psychologically, a catalyst must emerge. We first note the haphazard (unconscious) manner in how the three came together and also, the caution assigned to the role of the Bratwurst (who was "supposed to cook"). This is contrasted by the roles of the Mouse ( who was to "carry water, light the fire, and set the table") and the Bird (who was to "fly into the forest daily and fetch the wood") which are clearly stated. Added to the energy of *concern*, we now become aware that the direction for movement in the tale must be to find a fourth.

## Characters

In this Fairy Tale, there are three main characters; the **Little Mouse**, the **Little Bird,** and the **Bratwurst**. Each has assigned roles for supporting the peaceful and prosperous household. Significant to these three characters is that the bird and the mouse are naturally occurring in everyday existence, but the Bratwurst is not. The Bratwurst is created by humans, not naturally occurring.

The **Little Mouse**, whose skill set revolves around the Hestian principles of caring for the family by maintaining the hearth (lighting the fire), keeping order (setting the table), and securing the life force (carrying water), provides the feminine energies of nurturance, structure, and security in the tale.

On the other hand, **Little Bird** provides the masculine energies of this tale. His work is to leave the home, fly into the forest and fetch wood. His work of going out into the world and returning to the home provides for the necessary expansion of the family unit. As such, even his return, with the challenge for each changing their assigned roles, brings about the catalytic movement away from the stagnation of which they had been unaware. Like Prometheus, stealing the fire from the Gods, Little Bird is constantly moving his family unit toward greater consciousness.

**Bratwurst**, a type of hot dog, illustrates by its phallic representation, the life force via the energy of the masculine—sexuality, temporary desire, and enthusiasm. In the tale, he flirts with the cooking pot, jumping/swimming in and out four times to flavor the broth. With this playful manner of flirtation, his influence is short-lived. Psychologically, we know early in the tale by his inauthentic role that his influence will be temporary. As the tale progresses, we learn of the destruction of Bratwurst when the **dog** eats him because of the "false papers," which provide evidence of his long-standing deception. Yet, even in his deception, he overtly provides a representation of the wholeness dynamic with the four times each day that he jumps in and out of the soup. His unconscious/innocence of what he provides for the threesome does end up costing him his life, as he has carried "false papers" which justified the dog in eating him.

# Depth Psychology Analysis

From my commentary, the anatomy of "Concerning the Little Bird, the Little Mouse, and the Bratwurst" has been explained, so now, I am going to move into an alchemical analysis of the archetypal symbols experienced through the imagination that recognizes the vibrational sciences of sacred geometry, numerology, color, chakras, and spirituality.

Additional characters necessary for moving the plot include the **Bird in the forest** who provokes the Little Bird of the title, causing him to no longer be content. The instruction of this bird is the catalyst often found in a *shadow figure.* The energy of the shadow here brings forth, into consciousness, aspects of life for the Little Bird that he had never before encountered or considered for his existence. This catalytic shadow bird is feminine, because she is the anima figure for Little Bird and, hence, is representing his feminine nature. Our quest to find the fourth character is now complete. Attention can now be paid to the *alchemical* need for fire, for the heat to increase, so transformation can occur.

## Supporting Characters and Their Symbolism

The **woods/forest** represent a place of transformation where nature and spirit come together. Not surprisingly, we find our Shadow energy—the Bird in the forest—in the woods. Alchemically, this shadow bird is the catalyst for transformation potential.

The **dog,** being true to its nature as a protecter for the family unit, ate Bratwurst, explaining to Little Bird that he found false papers on him and, therefore, Bratwurst had to forfeit his life. Also, *consummation* (eating) represents the sacrament of communion and the processes of ingestion, digestion, and the return to the *prima materia,* the beginning of the alchemical process. Water is an implied necessary basic element found in alchemy and in each of the above-listed processes. Aware of Bratwurst's deceit by his possession of false papers (a misrepresentation of the Self), the Dog as a protector for the family unit fulfills his and Bratwurst's destinies. Bratwurst's deceit was taking on the false persona of a cook and *playing* with that role. By *playing* with the role of the cook, he was not living his authentic life. You will recall in the first paragraph of this tale, we became aware of the deceitful nature of Bratwurst when we learned he was "supposed" to cook.

In addition, the appearance of a Dog in a tale reminds us of its mythological role in human mortality. We have from Greek mythology, Cerberus (the five-headed dog) guarding the entrance to the underworld; from Egyptian mythology, Anubis (the jackal-headed dog/God) as an underworld guide; and from a Native American belief, dogs influenced God in making humans mortal, rather than granting them immortality. Alchemically, this interaction between Bratwurst and the Dog provides an example of the first stage in the alchemical process (the *prima materia)* which is represented by the color black.

The **cooking pot** is fueled/heated by both the wood brought by the Little Bird and the fire and water provided by the Little Mouse. In this manner, they unconsciously support the deception of Bratwurst as a "cook." Paradoxically, he brings the number four, the number of wholeness, to the story with the times he jumps in and out of the broth. In addition, we have an image of the container (Cooking Pot) which, from alchemy and from the psychological work of individuation, provides the boundaries necessary for the work of the transformation process. Now, we are aware of the energies of both the masculine (Little Bird) and the feminine (Little Mouse) as they provide necessary elements and balance. Once they take on the new unfamiliar roles, for which they are not suited, the balance is lost. As a result, Bratwurst has already lost his life to the Dog. By jumping into the cooking pot, Little Mouse loses her hair, skin, and, ultimately, her life. In the chaos that ensues, Little Bird falls into the well with the bucket and dies. This second stage of the alchemical process, is recognized as the color white and symbolized by the vessel/cooking pot.

**Fire** can alert the astute reader to the fact that changes are forthcoming. Fire— represented by heat, embers, flame, and blaze—can symbolize sexuality, procreation, and the alchemical element of sulfur. Fire, in its experience of combustion, requires air and heat. Literally, in our tale, the fire is fueled by the wood brought by Little Bird and stoked (air) by Little Mouse. Metaphorically, Little Bird brings the catalytic heat/flame into the family unit, when he accepts the challenge from his shadow bird, forcing a transformational chain of events. At the end of the tale, confusion results when Little Bird is not able to find the new cook (Little Mouse), as she has met her death in the cooking pot. In the chaos that ensues, Little Bird throws the wood about, which catches on fire and starts a non-contained blaze.

The final image we have is of Little Bird drowning with the bucket in the well when he tries to get water—the energy of the life force—to put out the blaze. This imagery recognizes that, yet again, a vessel for containment (the bucket) is not able to fulfill its function due to the chaotic behavior of Little Bird. The harmony that our threesome were living out of at the beginning this tale has been lost due to the catalytic influence causing reassigned roles for which each character was not well suited. This completes the life-death transformation process of all three main characters. The images here represent the third stage in the alchemical process, known as the fire heating up the contents in the vessel and recognized as the color yellow.

Just as fire has been evident from the beginning of the tale, so has the element of **water.** Water is both life giving and life taking, as we have seen. In our tale, Little Mouse, representing the feminine, meets her transformation/death in the waters of the cooking pot. Little Bird drowns by falling into the well with the bucket. The cooking pot, the bucket, and the well are all containers for water found in the tale. Water, by its nature, is mercurial as it can exist in many forms—solid, liquid, gas, and plasma.

Now that all three main characters are dead, they have entered into the fourth alchemical stage represented by the color red. As such, the life-death-life process continues as we will see below in the section on alchemical processes.

## Sacred Geometry

The two dominant images from sacred geometry for this tale are the tetrahedron, representing fire and the cube, representing the earth. Throughout this tale, fire has been ever present and requiring the support of the masculine and the feminine energies. The earth, represented by the transformational energies of the forest/woods and the energy found in the root chakra promoted the life-death-life experiences of our main characters.

## Numerology

Our tale begins with three characters, alerting us to the notion that a fourth character must emerge in order for wholeness to be manifest. As mentioned earlier, the number for wholeness, four, is overtly presented by the Bratwurst as he "coiled himself four times through the soup…"

## Colors

In our tale, "Concerning the Little Mouse, the Little Bird, and the Bratwurst," colors do not play a primary role. However, as with the numerology, we will see the color representations of alchemical significance in the section on alchemical processes.

## Chakras

The primary chakra represented in this tale is the first or Root Chakra. This chakra is known for its connection to the earth and survival. As the location for the home of life force energy (kundalini), it supports our tale's life-death-life experiences.

## The Alchemical Processes

Jungian archetypes can be understood or conceptualized as "organs" of the Psyche. As such, how does the alchemical process support the evolution of consciousness and, therefore, individuation? Jung experienced the alchemical process as analogous to modern-day psychoanalysis. His associations to the four major processes of alchemy were to see *nigredo* as the Shadow, *albedo* referring to the anima and animus (contra-sexual soul images), *citrinitas* as the wise old man (or woman) archetype, and *rubedo* as the Self archetype which has achieved wholeness.

We now enter into the discussion supporting alchemical significance in our tale. It is important to recognize the profound difficulty of presenting alchemical concepts in a linear fashion. Alchemy is multifaceted and holographic; therefore, one must keep in mind that *the processes occur simultaneously*. The Axiom of Maria Prophetissa— "One becomes two, two becomes three, and out of the third comes the one as the fourth"—is beneficial to recognize as a linear process *within* multifaceted-holographic experiences. This Axiom may be the most important revelation to grasp—**the significance of alchemical symbolism in Fairy Tales and, therefore, in the psychological process of individuation.** In Fairy Tales, as in individuation, it is important to be aware of both polarizations and transcendence.

What are the images found in our tale representing the stages of consciousness explored alchemically, and how do they support an individuation journey?

*Nigredo*—Prima materia—**Black:** The shadow bird, in alerting Little Bird to the potential of living a different life, heralds the appearance of the dog. Remember the role of the **dog** in sniffing out the deception of the sausage. Both in our tale and in myths, most literally, what is eaten will be digested and as an end product of digestion, produce the compost for new growth/life. Excrement is referred to as the color black and containing all potential. In the beginning, there is the **ONE**— the *prima materia*—the beginning of the alchemical/individuation process.

*Albedo*—Vessel—**White:** The **cooking pot** is a container for the opposites to come together, and therefore, a new creation to emerge from their union. Alchemically, these opposites are recognized as the energies of the masculine and the feminine. We can now recognize the number **TWO** from our Axiom—

setting up the feminine energy of Little Mouse and the masculine energies of Little Bird and Bratwurst.

*Citrinitas*—Heat—**Yellow**—Wisdom: The knowledge and energy to undergo and endure a transformational process is brought forward by the dynamic of **fire**. Fire that represents passion and desire, as well as, the fire that contains heat and burning flames of combustion, symbolizes this process of individuation. In our tale, the desire to change and take on new roles is evident. Also, the flames that get out of control, cause the ultimate experience—death of Little Bird. Similarly, death for Little Mouse occurs when the container became contaminated by her ignorance (lack of wisdom). These events support the number **THREE** from our Axiom. The masculine (bird) and feminine (mouse) are combined with the catalytic energy provided by the shadow bird in the forest. Thus, the fire which consumed the Little Mouse and the water which downed the Little Bird provided for their transformation—their evolution of consciousness, moving them beyond innocence.

*Rubedo*—Transformation—**Red:** Now all three characters have entered into the stage of death supporting the life-death-life (**water**) transformational structure of wholeness. The next stage will be a return to the **ONE** (new life) as demonstrated in the Maria Prophetissa's Axiom as **"…and out of the third comes the one as the FOURTH."** Having lost their innocence/life, the characters in our tale are now ready for the next stage of conscious evolution.

## Spirituality in the Fairy Tale

Spirituality is about finding a purpose or meaning to life. Our threesome moved out of innocence in order to live life more fully—with consciousness, and ultimately with an awareness of the dynamic of co-creation. Our threesome died to bring forward an opportunity to be **resurrected** into a new level of evolved consciousness and assistance in finding a life with meaning. By confronting the consequences of their death of ignorance, they now have returned to the *prima materia*, bringing into it a new dimension of conscious potential. Humanity grows in consciousness on the shoulders of those preceding us. Meaning flourishes within the opportunity of co-creation, rather than living a life of only innocence and ignorance. Co-creation is the process—within psyche, spirit, and matter—influencing the consciousness of both the individual and the Divine.

In our tale, as the threesome live an idyllic existence ignorant of the fullness of life, they are vulnerable to failures resulting from their innocence. They must—and do—die from the exclusive either/or existence and now can be resurrected into an opportunity for both/and lives more fully expressed (more consciously evolved).

The reader must remember that all Fairy Tales, at their core, illuminate different aspects of the evolutionary process of consciousness. To move into the both/and, we do not dissolve the either/or; we learn to grow *through* polarizations. This growth through, what Jung refers to as the tension of opposites, is what allows us to evolve.

# CHAPTER 4

# 1

# The Frog King or Iron Henry

Translated from the original German version of the Grimms Fairy Tale collection.

# I

# The Frog King or Iron Henry[30]

In the old times when wishing still helped[31] lived a king whose daughters were all beautiful, but the youngest was so beautiful that the sun, itself, which had seen so much, marveled whenever it shone in her face. Close by the king's castle lay a great, dark forest and in the forest, under an old linden tree,[32]

---

[30] **The Frog King or Iron Henry** -- Der Froschkönig oder der Eiserne Heinrich. The title is a literal translation.

[31] **When wishing still helped** - wo das Wünschen noch geholfen hat, a literal translation.

The reference to "wishing" here seems enigmatical. Jung

speaks of "the originally magical significance of the word 'wish,' which . . . expresses not just wishing in the sense of desire but a magical action, and the traditional belief in the efficacy of prayer" ("Synchronicity: An Acausal Connecting Principle," CW 8, ,l 966 and n. 16). He also comments that "God is our own longing [wishing?] to which we pay divine honors" (Psychology of the Unconscious, 1916, p. 96.).

In "The Three Feathers" (63.), the toad that helps the youngest son is called an Itsche in the German text. While this may be an obscure dialect term for toad, in Sanskrit--and German belongs to the Indo-Germanic language group--itscha means "wishing" or "desire." The dumbling's openness to what he encounters in "Three Feathers" proves to be his salvation. In other words, he was able to accept the help of "wishing." In more pro saic language, one could say, "In olden times, when there was still an openness to magic or the unconscious . . ."

[32] **Linden tree** - The linden is a European variety of the basswood family. It is best known, perhaps, to Americans from the avenue in Berlin, Unter den

was a well. When the day was very warm, the king's child went out into the forest and sat herself on the edge of the cool well. And when she was bored, she took a golden ball[33] and threw it up high and caught it again. And it was her favorite plaything.

Now it once came to pass that the king's daughter's golden ball did not fall into her little hand, which she held up high, but hit the earth nearby and rolled straight into the water. The king's daughter followed it with her eyes, but the ball disappeared and the well was deep, so deep that one could not see the bottom. Then she began to cry and cried louder and louder and could find no solace. And as she thus lamented, someone called to her, "What's up with you, king's daughter? You shriek so that even a stone would feel pity." She looked around to see where the voice came from and caught sight of a frog stretching its thick, ugly head out of the water. "Oh, it's you, old water-splasher," she said. "I am weeping for my golden ball which has fallen down into the well." -- "Be still and do not weep," answered the frog. "I can figure something out, but what will you give me if I bring your plaything back up?" -- "Whatever you will have, dear frog," she said, "my clothes, my pearls and precious stones, even the golden crown, which I wear." The frog answered, "Your clothes, your pearls and precious stones, and

---

Linden, which is lined with these trees. In German folklore, the lin den is the quintessential tree of German Romanticism and is almost always found with a spring or water source. It is the feminine representative of the tree world by contrast with the oak, which was sacred to Wotan.

[33] **Ball** - Kugel, "ball," "globe," or "sphere." Although a Kugel is a ball, it also carries wider imaginal connotations than simply, "ball."

your golden crown I do not care for. But if you will like me and I can be your companion and playmate, sit next to you at your little table, eat from your little golden plate, drink out of your little cup, and sleep in your little bed, if you promise me this I will climb down and bring you up the golden ball again." -- "Oh, yes," she said. "I promise you everything that you want if you will only bring me back my ball." But she thought, "How the simple frog talks! He sits in the water with those like him and croaks and can be no companion to any human being!"

The frog, when he had received her agreement, dipped his head under [the water], sank down, and in a little while came rowing up again, had the ball in his mouth, and threw it into the grass. The king's daughter was filled with joy when she saw her beautiful play thing again, picked it up, and ran off with it. "Wait, wait," called the frog. "Take me along. I can't run like you." But what did it help him to cry his "croak, croak" after her as loudly as he could! She did not listen, hurried home, and had soon forgotten the poor frog, who had to climb down into his well again.

The next day when she had seated herself with the king and all the people of the court at table and was eating from her little golden plate, there came, splish splash, splish splash, something crawling up the marble stairs. When it had reached the top, it knocked at the door and cried, "King's daughter, youngest [one], open for me." She ran and wanted to see who might be outside, but when she opened the door, there sat the frog in front of it. Then she hastily threw the door shut, sat down at the table again, and was most afraid. The king saw clearly that her heart was beating violently and said, "My child, what are you afraid of? Is there maybe a giant standing at the door and wants to fetch you?" -- "Oh, no," she answered, "it is no giant, but a disgusting frog." -- "What does the frog want of you?" "Oh, dear father, when I was in the forest yesterday, sitting by the well and playing, my golden ball fell into the water. And because I cried so, the frog brought it up again, and because he so insisted, I promised him he should be my companion. I never ever thought he would be able to come up out of his water! Now he is outside and wants to come into me." There upon came a second knock and the cry,

*"King's daughter, youngest [one},*
*Open for me.*
*Do not you know what yesterday*
*You said to me*
*By the cool water of the well?*
*King's daughter, youngest [one},*
*Open for me! "[34]*

---

[34] "Königstochter, jüngste,
Mach mir auf,
Weißt du nicht, was gestern
Du zu mir gesagt
Bei dem kühlen Brunnenwasser?
Königstochter, jüngste,
Mach mir auf"

Then the king said, "What you have promised, that must you keep. Go and open for him." She went and opened the door and the frog hopped in after her, step by step, to her chair. There he sat and called, "Lift me up to you." She hesitated until at last the king ordered it. As soon as the frog was on the chair, he wanted on the table, and when he sat there he said, "Now shove your little golden plate nearer to me so that we [can] eat together." She did so, but one saw clearly that she did not do it gladly. The frog ate heartily, but almost every little bite caught in her throat.

Finally he said, "I have eaten my fill and am tired. Now carry me to your little bedroom[35] and make ready your little silken bed so we can lie down to sleep." The king's daughter began to cry and she was afraid of the cold frog which she did not dare to touch and which was now supposed to sleep in her pretty, clean[36] little bed. But the king became angry and said, "He who helped you when you were in need should you not hereafter despise." So she grabbed him with two fingers, carried him up[stairs], and set him in a comer. But when she lay in bed, he crawled [to her] and said, "I am tired. I want to sleep as well as you: lift me up or I will tell your father." At this she became furious, picked him up, and threw him against the wall with all her might. "Now you will have rest, you vile frog."

---

[35] **bedroom** -- *Kammer*, "chamber," "room." Although the text does not read *Bettkammer*, "bedchamber," that is the implication.

[36] **clean** -- *rein*, which carries the connotation of "pure" or "purity", rather than just "free of dirt."

When, however, he fell [to the ground], he was no frog but a king's son with beautiful and friendly eyes. He was now, according to her father's will, her dear companion and husband. Then he told her he had been enchanted by a wicked witch, and no one could have re leased him from the well but she, alone, and in the morning they would go together to his kingdom. Then they went to sleep and the next morning when the sun awakened them, a carriage came driving up drawn by eight white horses, which had white ostrich feathers on their heads and went with golden chains. At the rear stood the young king's servant: it was faithful Henry. Faithful Henry had been so unhappy when his master was changed into a frog that he had had three iron bands laid around his heart so that it should not burst from woe and sadness. The carriage was to carry the young king to his king dom. Faithful Henry lifted them both in, took his place at the rear, and was full of joy over this deliverance. And when they had traveled a part of the way, the king's son heard it crack behind him as if some thing had broken. He turned around and cried,

*"Henry, the carriage is breaking."*
*"No, master, not the carriage.*
*It is a band from my heart,*
*Which lay in great pain*
*When you sat in the well*

*When you were a frog."* [37]

Again and yet again there was a crack along the way, and each time the king's son thought the carriage was breaking, and it was only the bands that sprang from the heart of faithful Henry because his master was released and happy.

*translated by Gary V Hartman*
*© 1991 Gary V Hartman*

---

[37] "Heinrich, der Wagen bricht."
"Nein, Herr, der Wagen nicht,
Es ist ein Band von meinem Herzen,
Das da lag in groj3en Schmerzen,
Als [hr in dem Brunnen saj3t,
Als !hr eine Fretsche wast."

I have translated this for the meaning and not for the rhymed couplets of the original.
Except for this last verse, whenever "frog" is mentioned in the story, the German word is Frosch. Here, however, the word is Fretsche, a dialect term for "frog," perhaps suggesting Remy's down-to-earth quality and/or servant status.

*Illustration by Audrey Leamon*

## Artist's Comments

It was such a surprise to read the original version of <u>The Frog Prince</u>. In the Disney version of course, the story has been romanticized to the point that the maiden kissing the frog seems more like a good deed. The moral of which is "be kind to those who look froggy (warts and all) and in the long run you will be rewarded."

In reality, the story tells us, you have a right to declare "enough already!" and to cease giving in to this obnoxious creature and his nagging demands even to the point of violence which, in the long run, released him to be his true self.

The character of "Iron Henry" seemed to me to be both a mentor and an alter ego which is why I chose to represent him as a silhouette; large and looming, but watching over all.

# #1

## The Frog King, or Iron Henry Commentary and Analysis

Lois Wilkins, PhD, APRN

# Commentary

This commentary honors the wisdom found in "The Frog King, or Iron Henry," as we understand its importance to the individuation process, which is, from a depth psychology perspective, the movement of a person toward wholeness. The Frog King alerts the reader to the archetypal influences found in the individuation process. This process of individuation reflects the quaternary structure found in the psyche represented by the personal unconscious, the collective unconscious, the ego, and the Self. Within each of these, we find the complexes, the shadow, the anima and animus energies, and the persona fulfilling the self-regulating process that is the overt function of psyche. What is unique about this Fairy Tale is the recognition that both royalty and human expression have equal importance in the tale. Therefore both alchemical influences through royalty and mundane life experience through Iron Henry will be encountered.

Recognizing that Fairy Tales mirror the psychological process of individuation, the following quote from von Franz's 1978, *Interpretation of Fairy Tales,* informs us:

> Fairy tales are the purest and simplest expression of collective unconscious psychic processes. Therefore their value for the scientific investigation of the unconscious exceeds that of all other material. They represent the archetypes in their simplest, barest, and most concise form. In this pure form, the archetypal images afford us the best clues to the understanding of the processes going on in the collective psyche. In myths or legends, or any other more elaborate mythological material, we get at the basic patterns of the human psyche through an overlay of cultural material. But in fairy tales there is much less specific conscious cultural material, and therefore they mirror the basic patterns of the psyche more clearly. (p.1)

## Title

What does it mean that we are given two titles to the same story? Often this tale carries the title of "The Frog King," alerting the reader to the journey to be encountered by one character, the Frog King. One must keep in mind that in terms of the transformation journey, the King must first be a Prince, otherwise recognized in this tale as the young King. By the use of its additional title of "Iron Henry," the reader is alerted to the awareness, not only of the alchemical royal journey but, also, the everyday journey of a human. This holds significance as many Fairy Tales stay in one domain or the other, that of royalty or that of everyday life. Therefore, our dual title recognizes the presence of potential growth in both domains.

To be consistent with Hartman's translation, you will note throughout my commentary and analysis that when not specifically using the term the "Frog King," I am using the term, the "young King." It is because of my understanding that what is contained in this Frog is a kingship, because he carries the knowledge of how to have his spell broken, he seeks out a wise King, inferring that his own father, for whatever reason is not available to him. In this Fairy Tale, we have two frames of reference for the story. Iron Henry speaks of a man of strength (Iron) and the Frog King speaks to an unusual type of King, a King enchanted by a wicked witch to live out of the body of a frog. So we know from the title that there will be two main male figures of importance in this story—one from a base earthly instinctual nature, the other from a tempered strength. At the very beginning, in the title, the alchemical elements of earth, fire, water, air, and ether are represented—earth with our frog, fire and air with the tempering of iron, water with the living environment of the frog, and ether with the notion of the enchanted Frog King.

The "Frog King" portion of the title alerts the reader to the dynamics of fertility and emerging sexuality. We know this because of the psychological symbolism of frog, which is assigned to the male genitalia (the scrotum).

Knowing the title represents the core themes to be found in the tale, one of the most profound issues will be that of grief and how it comes to be transformed.

So, psychologically, two aspects of the masculine are primed for transformation: first, the aspect of the grieving servant having experienced the loss of his master through the enchantment that turned him into a frog; and second, the young King, thereby, cloaked in the body of the frog.

## The Initial Paragraph

In this first paragraph, we notice that there is not a Queen as we are only told of the **King** and his daughters. Alchemically, evidence that magic will find its way into our story occurs with the use of the etherial term, "wishing." The presence of a **"well"** tells us that this will be a journey of depth in relationship to the individuation process. Innocence is represented by the **Princess** "playing," not attending to serious life issues. The **"golden ball"** gives us our first encounter with wholeness and color. In this case, golden is representative of great wealth. The ball, a sphere/globe, in the original German a *kugel,* alerts the reader that this specific ball also carries wider imaginal connotations and that the story will end with the fulfillment of wholeness. The golden sun shining brightly on her face is another representation of wealth, a wealth that is not worldly.

## Main Characters

The **Frog King** is encumbered with what will be seen as a false persona. A **Wicked Witch** forced the false persona of the frog upon him, at which time she also pronounced the cure that would break the spell. This false persona of the Frog was intended to relegate the Frog King to a most base instinctual level of existence. By grace, the Frog King had the use of his more advanced intellect and knew the Princess' father, a wise King, would be able to assist him. The Frog King knew that he needed to woo or seduce the Princess in order to have the spell broken, which would allow him to claim both his Queen and his Kingship/Kingdom.

Here we see the Princess facing challenges as she moves from innocence toward maturity, i.e., from a Princess to a Queen. She must learn to honor her word which, lucky for her, she has a wise father, the King, who demands this of her. Her repulsion of the frog is not unlike the unbidden changes that come in adolescence. Her frustration, when she finds no escape from the Frog's pursuits, results in an aggressive, physically abusive action, as when she throws the Frog against the wall. Here, the **wall** represents a boundary that cannot be avoided. No longer playing with the destiny of her wholeness, represented by the golden ball retrieved by the Frog King, she intentionally throws the metaphorical ball (the Frog King) against the wall, manifesting wholeness for both herself and the Frog King. Was it her emerging sexuality? As the Fairy Tale reveals, what was repulsive to her, what she has resisted, is now the handsome King of her dreams.

The young King, now free from his Frog persona, explained what had happened to him and is forever devoted and grateful to the Princess/Queen for his freedom and his Kingship. Her father, the King, declares them married, thereby fulfilling her task of becoming a Queen. **Iron Henry**, the young King's faithful servant, brings the carriage with eight horses wearing white ostrich feathers and golden chains to take the newlyweds to their Kingdom.

With the acceptance of her King, the receptive/feminine aspects of the psyche have come into balance. In the beginning of our story, the Princess was all about getting everything she wanted and not giving anything. She had to endure a crisis in order to move her energy out, which occurred when she threw the Frog against the wall. We could say what would have been a complex of repressed sexuality was resolved through a violent encounter with the "wall." This encounter was her confrontation with the unmovable wall of physical, sexual maturation. In other words, kids grow up.

## Other Characters and Symbolism of Images

All of the characters in the story work toward the maturation of the Princess becoming a Queen, which is what we learned in our first paragraph. As we continue to explore the supporting characters and symbols of our tale, I will show the multidimensionality in the evolution of consciousness both from the collective and personal realms. The reader must be vigilant about the multidimensionality of a single image. It cannot be overstated that the perception of images in the realm of subtle energies, involves the senses of sight/vision, touch, taste, sound, smell, and intuition.

The **carriage**, powered by the horses, is the vehicle of motion to carry the once Frog King and Princess, now King and Queen, into their new lives. The recognition of the infinity symbol, represented in both the **number "eight"** and the wheels on the carriage, symbolically informs us of their combined destinies. The carriage, metaphorically, can be seen as a human body in that it now carries the energies of both the masculine and the feminine. Separately, in the outer world, our tale has told us of the energies of the masculine and the feminine now united in the carriage. The horses, symbolically, represent the power of an individuals growth of self-esteem. This ability to move beyond assigned roles is a function of the individuation process.

The **Wicked Witch** is acknowledged as putting the spell on the young King, which turned him into a frog and also giving him the ability to undo the spell. This is an example of the collective unconscious contaminating and overwhelming the movement toward conscious expression. Any spell or curse exists in the realm of the subtle energy of spirit/ether. Through this realm of subtle energy vibrations, the Wicked Witch *wills* the young King into a frog. She does not physically touch him for this transformation to occur. Through the powers of her energies, she has the abilities through spirit (ether) for this regressive transformation to occur. This is not unlike the psychological collusion that must occur with the dynamic of scapegoating. On some level, just as an individual must collude with the perpetrator of a scapegoating dynamic, the young King required the regression of becoming the frog.

When the King heard the sound of what he thought was the carriage breaking, with the **Iron Bands** releasing from Iron Henry's heart, it was, in fact, an opening to a new dimension of freedom for Iron Henry, the human in this tale. There is also a trinity dynamic in which each of these three bands breaks. The breaking of each band can be seen as releasing time/space bondage and supporting the infinity dynamic of no longer being restricted by past, present, and future. This movement beyond the time-space continuum recognizes infinity as an alchemical goal of fulfillment with destiny. The destiny for Iron Henry was to be released from his grief once the young King was free of the enchantment/curse. Grief when explored is recognition of love that has no place to go. Now the love that Iron Henry feels for his King has it proper place and can expressed.

Now, let's look at the symbolism of the **frog**. As stated earlier, the frog symbolizes masculine sexuality, specifically the scrotum and the instinct of procreation. Frogs also denote aspects of cleansing; they speak of new life and harmony. They are examples of the energy of water with its ability to refresh, purify, and replenish. In our tale, we know there is a need for replenishment, in order for the young King to manifest his Queen and kingdom. The young King, through his experience of enchantment by the Wicked Witch, is forced into a regressive, in fact, a reptilian experience. This is significant, psychodynamically, if we allow the role of the Lilith side of the archetypal mother to bestow such a curse/enchantment upon the young King. What we do know is that the result of this was a forced evolutionary regression to the reptile. Therefore, it could be implied that our young King was, at some level, precocious. By that I mean, he was behaving in a manner that was not justified by his level of maturation. This theme of false maturity, precociousness, is one we will encounter in other Fairy Tales.

The **well** is an example of feminine energy and also illustrates the co-creation between nature and humanity, since a human must build something in order to reach water (nature). In our story, we have a deep well, evidence of connection to the underworld—our own unknown reflective depths mirroring the psychic multidimensionality, much like a house of mirrors projects infinity. People wish upon a well in the hope of having desires fulfilled, recognizing a wide range of feelings-imagination-dreams-ideas. Some universal attributes of wells include: being connected to the Earth Mother; an image of nurturance; in Hebrew language, the word for well has the meaning of woman or bride; welling up from the depths of the earth; earth/water/air; sources of plenty and of life; a symbol of secrecy. In addition, an uncovered well with a good supply of water is a symbol of good fortune. In our story, for both the Frog and the Princess, truth is to be found at the bottom of the well, which is all about the wholeness of their individuation processes.

The next image is the spherical golden **ball**, which we have noted earlier as a symbol of wholeness. The Princess has it in her hands, she loses it, and the Frog retrieves it for her. The ball is symbolic of a marriage of Heaven and Earth, and at the most mundane level, of a man and a woman, as the ball is the cubing of a circle. The wholeness of heaven and earth, the human and divine, the bridge between heaven and earth are captured in this symbol of wholeness that is a ball. In our story, just as our young King lost his wholeness when enchanted/cursed by the Wicked Witch, our Princess has lost possession of her wholeness by losing the golden ball. Due to the frog King's retrieval, the wholeness that was theirs individually can now be united.

A rich symbol of life is that of a **forest.** The darkness of the forest and the deep roots of its trees symbolize the unconscious so, being on the edge of the forest, which is where our tale takes place, is representative of the potential for emerging consciousness. The regressive move forced upon the young King and the resistance of the Princess to honor her promise show the two dynamics that need to be brought to consciousness in order to evolve. Fairy tales often take place at the edge of a forest, helping us to understand the psychological significance of evolving consciousness found in these tales.

The **carriage** is a vehicle for movement and another feminine figure as it is a container. The carriage holds the new King and Queen, as well as Iron Henry, the faithful servant of the young King.

**Iron Henry** is ever present as the King's faithful servant, and the significance of his power is indicated by his name, "Iron." Iron is necessary for vitality of the life force. With such a faithful servant, our young King is never at risk of losing his life force. Historically, the Frog King's faithful servant, "Iron Henry," is defending against his heart being fatally broken through the depth of his sorrow and grief. This has often been expressed in ancient poetry and folklore as a heart being kept in bands. In the case of our tale, the use of iron bands would be to emphasize the strength needed to hold his heart together.

There are eight **horses** to pull the carriage. Horses symbolize power and strength, as in horse power. Once again, we see the significance of destiny through the number of horses (eight), representing infinity. In our tale, the quaternary structure of wholeness for the feminine is represented by the Queen, and the quaternary structure of wholeness for the masculine is represented by the King. This wholeness is symbolically represented by the eight horses pulling their carriage. True personal power is the wisdom obtained from walking your own journey. The young King had to find his way to a receptive

Princess, while the Princess had to be confronted by her failure to live up to her promise. In this way, they both were required to walk their own journey before they could be united.

**Chains** laced around the wheels of the carriage are a symbol of binding together parts of a whole. In our story, they reinforce the coming together of the King and Queen in marriage. The image of a chain, a length of entwined circles is, in and of itself, a powerful representation of wholeness. Psychologically, scientifically, and in terms of humanity, we now have knowledge of the double-helix DNA/RNA chains that manifest physical/biological destiny.

At the end of our tale, the eight horses are adorned with **ostrich feather** headpieces. These magical protective totems can be seen as protection from harmful magic like that of the Wicked Witch. Therefore, our King and Queen move into their kingdom with safety provided by these ostrich feather totems.

# Depth Psychology Analysis

From my commentary, the anatomy of "The Frog King or Iron Henry" has been explained, so now, I am going to move into an alchemical analysis of the archetypal symbols experienced through the imagination that recognizes the vibrational sciences of sacred geometry, numerology, color, chakras, and spirituality.

To experience "The Frog King or Iron Henry" as its own representation of wholeness or Self, not unlike the wholeness of the Psyche, it is important to recognize with Hartman's translation of this Grimm's Fairy Tales, and my commentary and analyses, we will find many examples of wholeness and, therefore, infinity. The overt alchemical symbolism recognized through the sciences of vibrations are explored in this analysis multidimensionally.

## The Sacred Geometry

In the wholeness represented in every Fairy Tale, the overarching sacred geometric figure is that of the octahedron, as it is representative of the psyche, according to Carl Jung. The octahedron is a symbol of the *quarternio* which is also a symbol of wholeness. In all Fairy Tales, this Sacred Geometry is reflective of the wholeness found in both the self-regulating psyche and in an individuation journey.

Another significant figure of Sacred Geometry found in "The Frog King, or Iron Henry" is that of the dodecahedron. Of the five platonic solids in Sacred Geometry, the dodecahedron is the most spherical. It produces its spherical shape through its twelve flat surfaces, as shown in Figure 6. The dodecahedron symbol connects with the dynamic of the ether of spirit. In this tale, we are immediately introduced to the golden *ball* and its spherical shape and, at the end of our tale, the *wheels* of the carriage also reflect roundness. The *well* also implies roundness, as do the *iron bands* encircling the torso of Iron Henry.

As you read below in the section on numerology you will see how the numerological significance of the number twelve (12) promotes the sacred geometry of the dodecahedron and how it is chosen as the sacred geometrical symbol for this tale.

## Numerology

Numerology is found in the number twelve (12) the number eight (8), the number four (4), and the number three (3) in this tale.

The number eight, found with the eight horses pulling the carriage (representing the infinity symbol), is the number of cosmic balance. According to the Tarot, the infinity symbol is also the symbol of justice.

The number four found with the four wheels of the carriage indicates the connection with earth and, for the purpose of movement, the wheels, due to their circular shape, represent wholeness. The number four is a representation of what is solid and is the number of completion. The cosmology of Jungian thought and, therefore, depth psychology is based upon the fundamental significance attached to the number four. This quaternary structure is the archetypal basis of the human psyche, the wholeness represented by the balancing of masculine and feminine energies through the evolution of consciousness. Therefore, the number four also represents the totality of conscious and unconscious psychic processes. Support for Maria Prophetissa's fundamental alchemical axiom, "One becomes Two, Two becomes Three and out of the Third comes the One as the Fourth." For clarification, imagine a seed (One) putting down roots and producing a stem (Two), then producing leaves (Three) which then produces a blossom (Four) which, again, produces a seed (One).

The number three, represented by the three iron straps around Iron Henry's heart, is an expression of intellectual and spiritual order and past-present-future; therefore, it is about the movement of individuation. Freud viewed the number three as a sexual symbol, that of father-mother-child. Also the number three supports social order—infant-child-adult and home-town-nation. The number three is considered energetically as masculine, and this energy is what propels both the Princess and the Frog King in their journeys toward wholeness. In depth psychology terminology, the number three represents the energy of the animus for outward motion.

This dodecahedron is assigned as the sacred geometric representation for this tale through its numerological significance with the number twelve (12). For the dodecahedron found in this tale, there are four spherical representations—the ball the princess is playing with retrieved by the frog, the entrance to the well implied as circular, the wheels on the carriage, and the iron bands around the torso of Iron Henry.

## Chakras

All life forms have energy centers known in the human body as energy systems usually depicted as seven (7), that travel from the base of the spine to the top of the head. In this tale, we are most concerned with the first chakra, the center for Kundalini or primary life-force energy, and the fourth chakra, the heart chakra, the center for compassion. The chakra system uses a realm of sacred geometry. In some traditions, this scared geometry is represented by various configurations of the lotus. It is through the heart chakra of Iron Henry and through the root chakras survival instinct found in the young enchanted King and the Princess that allow for their individuation journeys and our recognition of these chakra influences.

## The Colors

The colors emphasized are gold and white, while green is implied from the frog and the forest. Gold (her ball and golden chains on the horses) represents the sun, masculine Zeus energies, as well as power, riches, both material and spiritual. White (horses and ostrich feathers) denotes the moon, the feminine, sacred, pure, and holy. Green brings forth the energies of growth and the life force.

## The Metals

The metal gold (the golden chains on the horses) is pure and of great value. The iron metal (around Iron Henry's heart) represents strength, endurance and the need for temperance. Therefore these two metals indicate pure strength of great value and endurance once tempered. The influence of being tempered by the experiences by life events shapes not only our tale but, also, the significance of these two metals in our recognition of the alchemical processes at play.

## Spirituality

Recognizing that none of the characters in our tale have names other than Iron Henry, indicates the generalizability of this tale. The tale is representative of each person's individuation journey—the journey toward wholeness.

In our tale, faith, a foundation of spirituality, was demonstrated by several factors: 1) the first King, with his wise insistence that his daughter honor her word, indicated his belief in a positive outcome in her relationship with herself and, ultimately, with the frog; 2) the Frog, knowing this Princess had the power to break the spell and become his Queen, retrieved the ball placing a symbol of wholeness back in his possession. He then proceeded to bring forth his many demands of the Princess; 3) the Princess by submitting to her father's, authority, relinquished her childhood, her willfulness; and 4) finally, Iron Henry, determined to not die from a broken heart, exemplifies the alchemical base metal of Iron. This tempering of the alchemist's lead, thereby enabled the transformational process of becoming the alchemist's gold—the Princess becoming the Queen and the Frog King overcoming the curse. In this manner, Iron Henry was catalytic for the individuation of all of them.

Take a moment to reflect on the illustration provided by Audrey Leamon at the beginning of this commentary and analysis. In his shadowy, almost ghost-like image, Iron Henry can be viewed as ever-present, an apt depiction for the spiritual dynamic of faith. Faith is the overriding spiritual principle of this tale.

# Notes/Figures

## Cover Image

This ancient alchemical image has been chosen in honor of the dynamic of transformational containment represented by the dragon in the vessel.

## Forward

[1]Jung, C. G. (1985). The practice of psychotherapy (Vol. 16)

(R. F. C. Hull, Trans.). Princeton:Princeton University

Press. (Original work published 1966).

**Figure 1:** *Rosario Philosophorum*

Sixteenth Century Floor Rosario philosophorum room,

(n.d.). Retrieved May 26, 2020 from
https://www.alchemywebsite.com/virtual_museum/rosarium_
philosophorum_room.html

[2]Fabricius, J. (1994). *Alchemy: The medieval alchemists and their royal art*. London: Diamond Books. (Original work published 1976).

[3]von Franz, M. L. (1974). *Number and time: Reflections leading toward a unification of depth psychology and physics* (Andrea Dykes, Trans.). Evanston: Northwestern University Press. (Original work published in 1970).

## Introduction

**Figure 2**: *Amphitheatrum sapient aeternae*

"Kneeling in his laboratory, an alchemist prays before a tabernacle inscribed, 'Happy the one who follows the advice of the Lord'; 'Do not speak of God without enlightenment'; 'When we attend strictly to our work God himself will helps." The inscription over the doorway at the far end of the sumptuous hall reads: 'While sleeping, watch!' Engraving 1604 designed by Heinrich Khunrath."

Fabricius, Johannes.(1994). *Alchemy: The medieval*

*alchemists and their royal art. (p. 7).* London: Diamond

Books. (Original work published in 1976)

**Figure 3**: *Tripus aureus*

"The vignette that is on the title-page to the *Tripus aureus* (1618) is a graphic illustration of the double face of alchemy. The picture is divided into two parts. On the right is a laboratory where a man, clothed only in trunks, is busy at the fire; on the left a library, where an abbot, a monk, and a layman are conferring together. In the middle, on top of the furnace stands the tripod with a round flask on it containing a winged dragon. The dragon symbolizes the visionary experience of the alchemist as he works in his laboratory and 'theorizes.'"

Jung, C. G. *The Collected Works of C. G. Jung, Vol 12,*

*Psychology and Alchemy,* trans. R. F C. Hull. (pp.

290-291). Princeton: Princeton University Press. 2nd ed.

(1968) 4th Printing 1977.

**Figure 4:** Imagination

Image: A Wendal graphic painting, created in collaboration with Dr. Lois E. Wilkins.

Wendal's graphic painting depicts, to the discerning eye, the multitude of vibrational sciences that make up alchemy.

In Spring 2002, an article I wrote an article published in the *The Journal of Poetry Therapy* titled, "Metaphorical language: Seeing and hearing with the heart." The recognition of metaphorical language is necessary in understanding the holographic multidimensionality of the imagination.

**Figure 5:** Metatron Cube

"The column of the centre is Metatron whose name is that of the Lord. It is created and constituted to be his image and likeness, and it includes all gradations from Above to Below and from Below to Above, and binds them together in the centre. *Fragmentarische Ausarbeitungen zur Anatomie* (Sudhoff, III, p. 462)."

Jung, C.G. (1978). *Aion: Researches into the phenomenology of the self.* (2nd ed., Vol. 9) (R. F. C. Hull, Trans.). Princeton: Princeton University Press. (Original work published 1951).

Image: Photographer unknown. Image retrieved 5/26/2020 from

https://www.bing.com/images/search?view=detailV2&ccid=D%2B9dAHC4&id=87DD9B1D139BD4717C654576AB29210AD202BFC9&thid=OIP.D-9dAHC4gfC4_KQVr-fsjwHaHa&mediaurl=http%3A%2F%2Fmedia-cache-ec0.pinimg.com%2F736x%2Fee%2F27%2Fd3%2Fee27d384f7a6fce3fa0414f91bbec02b.jpg&exph=512&expw=512&q=Sacred+Geometry+Cube&simid=607992555182031233&selectedindex=5&ajaxhist=0&vt=0&sim=11

**Figure 6:** Platonic solids

For more information on the Platonic solids and their relevance to Sacred Geometry, see Kryder's work:

Kryder, Renee (1990) *Gaia Matrix Oracle, V0l. II: Readings for Worlds, Major Arcan and Symbols* (p. 254) Mount Shasta, CA: Golden Point Productions

Image: Quora, Inc. (2019). "Platonic solids." Image retrieved 5/23/2020 from https://www.quora.com/If-you-had-to-contain-gas-in-a-platonic-solid-which-would-hold-the-pressure-better-in-a-hypothetical-case-that-the-gas-is-constantly-increasing-in-pressure.

**Figure 7:** *Pensée Chinoise*

*Image:* Granet © Albin Michel, 1936, 1968, p. 149. In von Franz, Marie-Louise, *Number and Time: Reflections*

*Leading toward a Unification of Depth Psychology and Physics.* (A. Dykes,Trans.). Chicago: Northwestern University Press, 1974. (p. 238).

**Figure 8:** The Alchemy of Color

"…color during the Middle Ages was also understood for its material, scientific, and medicinal properties. The manufacture of colored pigments and inks was part of the science of alchemy, the forerunner of modern chemistry. Concerned with the transformation of matter, alchemy was closely tied to artistic practice."

Getty Media. (October 14, 2016). The iris: Behind the scenes at the Getty. Retrieved 5/25/2020 from https://blogs.getty.edu/iris/video-the-alchemy-of-color/ (Artist unknown).

**Figure 9:** The Seven Chakras System

Image: A Wendal graphic painting created in collaboration with Dr. Lois E. Wilkins. This is a depiction of the human chakra energy system potential.

**Figure 10:** Co-Creation: Psyche's Multidimensionality

Image: An Anna Leamon painting, created in collaboration with Dr. Lois Wilkins

# Bibliography

Bak, P. (1996). *How nature works: The science of self-organized criticality*. New York: Springer-Verlag New York, Inc.

Belensky, M. F., Clinchy, B. M., Goldberger, R. R., & Tarule, J. M. (1986). *Women's ways of knowing: The development of self, voice, and mind*. NewYork: Basic Books.

Bergson, H. (1946). *Creative mind*. New York: Philosophical Library.

Bernheimer, K., Ed. (2010). *My mother she killed me, my father he ate me*. New York: Penguin Group.

Bettelheim, B. (1976). *The uses of enchantment: The meaning and importance of fairy tales*. New York: Alfred A. Knopf.

Bishop, P. (2002). *Jung's answer to Job: A commentary*. New York: Bruner Routledge.

Bohm, D. & Peat, F. (1987). *Science, order and creativity*. New York: Bantam *Books*.

Brown, J. (1961). *Freud and the post-freudians*. Baltimore: Penguin Books, Inc.

Campbell, J. (1968). *Hero with a thousand faces. (2nd ed.)*. Princeton, NJ: Princeton University Press.

Carotenuto, A. (1981). *The vertical labyrinth: Individuation in Jungian psychology*. Toronto: Inner City Books.

Carotenuto, A. (1982). *A secret symmetry:Sabina Spielrein between Jung and Freud.* (A. Pomerans, J. Shepley, & K. Winston, Trans.). New York: Pantheon Books.

Chevalier, T. (2004). *The lady and the unicorn.* New York: Penguin Group.

Citro, M. (2011). *The basic code of the universe: The science of the invisible in physics, medicine, and spirituality.* Rochester, VT: Park Street Press.

Corbett, L. (1996). *The religious function of the psyche.* London & New York: Routledge.

Cornwell, J. (Ed.). (1995). *Nature's imagination: The frontiers of scientific vision.* Oxford: Oxford University Press.

Currivan, J. (2017). *The cosmic hologram: In-formation at the center of creation.* Rochester, VT: Inner Traditions.

Davies, P., & Gribbin, J. (1992). *The matter myth: Dramatic discoveries that challenge our understanding of physical reality.* New York: Simon & Schuster /Touchstone.

de Saint Exupéry, A. (1971). *The Little Prince.* (K. Woods, Trans.). New York: Harcourt Brace Jovanovich, Publishers. (Original work published 1943).

Dyson, F. (1995). Introduction. In J. Cornwell (Ed.), *Nature's imagination: The frontiers of scientific vision.* Oxford: Oxford University Press.

Edelman, G. (1995). Memory and the individual soul: Against silly reductionism. In J. Cornwell (Ed.), *Nature's imagination: The frontiers of scientific vision* (pp. 200-206). Oxford: Oxford University Press.

Edinger, E. (1986). *Encounter with the self.* Toronto: Inner City Books.

Edinger, E. F. (1996). *The new God-image.* Wilmette, IL: Chiron Publications.

Estes, C. (1992). *Women who run with the wolves: Myths and stories of the wild woman archetype.* New York: Ballantine Books.

Fabricius, J. (1994). *Alchemy: The medieval alchemists and their royal art.* London: Diamond Books. (Original work published 1976).

Ferguson, M. (1985). Karl Pribram's changing reality. In Ken Wilber (Ed.), *The holographic paradigm and other paradoxes.* Boston & London: Shambhala.

Forsyth, K. (2015). *The Wild Girl.* New York: St. Martin's Press.

Foucault, M. (1971). Neitzsche, genealogy, and history. In D. F. Bouchard (Ed.), *Michael Foucault: Language, counter-memory, practice: Selected essay sand interviews* (pp. 139-164). New York: Cornell University Press.

Friedman, N. (1997). *The hidden domain: Home of the quantum wave function, nature's creative source.* Eugene: The Woodbridge Group.

Fry, S. (1995). Science as Problem Solving. In A. Ornery, C. Kasper, & G. Page (Eds.), *In search of nursing science* (pp. 72-80). Thousand Oaks: Sage.

Fry, S. (2017). *Mythos: The Greek myths reimagined.* San Francisco: Chronicle Books.

Gleick, J. (1987). *Chaos: Making a new science.* New York: Penguin Books.

Gould, J. (2005). *Spinning straw into gold: What fairy tales reveal about the transformations on a woman's life.* New York: Random House.

Hampden-Turner, C. (1982). *Maps of the mind: Charts and concepts of the mind and its labyrinths.* New York: Collier Books.

Hand Clow, B. (2010). *Alchemy of nine dimensions: The 2011/2012 prophecies and nine dimensions of consciousness.* Charlottesville, VA: Hampton Roads Publishing. (Original work published, 2004.)

Herbert, N. (1985). *Quantum reality: Beyond the new physics.* Garden City: Anchor Press/Doubleday.

Hillman, J. (1972). *The myth of analysis.* New York: Northwestern University Press.

Hillman, J. (1975). *Re-visioning psychology.* New York: Harper & Row.

Hillman, J. (1981). *The thought of the heart.* Paper presented at Eranos Lectures, Dallas.

Hillman, J. (1983). *Archetypal psychology.* Dallas: Spring Publications. (Original work published 1981).

Hillman, J. (1983). *Healing fiction.* Dallas: Spring Publications.

Hillman, J. (1985). *Anima: An anatomy of a personified notion.* Dallas: Spring Publications.

Hillman, J. (Ed.). (1987). *Puer papers*. Dallas: Spring Publications.

Hillman, J. (1996). *The soul's code: In search of character and calling*. New York: Random House.

Hillman, J., & Shamdasani, S. (2013). *Lament of the Dead: Psychology after Jung's Red Book*. New York: W.W. Norton & Co.

Hoerni, U., Fischer, T., & Kaufmann, B., Eds. (2019). *The Art of C.G. Jung*. (P.D. Young & C. J Murray, Trans.). New York: W.W. Norton & Co.

Hundert, E. M. (1990). *Philosophy, psychiatry and neuroscience: Three approaches to the mind*. Oxford: Clarendon. (Original work published 1989).

Jacoby, M., Kast, V., and Riedel, I. (1992). *Witches, ogres, and the devil's daughter: Encounters with evil in fairy tales*. (M. H. Kohn, Trans.). Boston: Shambhala.

Jung, C. G. (1933). *Modern man in search of a soul* (C. Baynes, Trans.). London: Routledge & Kegan Paul. (Original work published 1928).

Jung, C. G. (1954). *Answer to Job*. United Kingdom: Routledge.

Jung, C. G. (1964). *Man and his symbols*. New York: Doubleday.

Jung, C. G. (1977). *Psychology and Alchemy*. (Rev. ed., Vol. 12) (R. F. C. Hull, Trans.). Princeton: Princeton University Press. (Original work published 1944).

Jung, C. G. (1977). *Two essays on analytical psychology* (2nd ed., Vol. 7). (R. F. C. Hull, Trans.). Princeton: Princeton University Press. (Original work published 1953).

Jung, C.G. (1978). *Aion: Researches into the phenomenology of the self.* (2nd ed., Vol. 9) (R. F. C. Hull, Trans.). Princeton: Princeton University Press. (Original work published 1951).

Jung, C. G. (1981). *The development of the personality* (Vol. 17) (R. F. C. Hull, Trans.). Princeton: Princeton University Press. (Original work published 1954).

Jung C. G. (1981). *The Structure and dynamics of the psyche* (2nd ed., Vol. 8) (R. F. C. Hull, Trans.). Princeton: Princeton University Press. (Original work published 1960)

Jung, C. G. (1983). *Alchemical studies* (Vol. 13) (R. F. C. Hull, Trans.). Princeton:Princeton University Press. (Original work published 1967).

Jung, C. G. (1985). *The practice of psychotherapy* (Vol. 16) (R. F. C. Hull, Trans.). Princeton:Princeton University Press. (Original work published 1966).

Jung, C. G. (1989). *Mysterium coniunctionis* (2nd ed., Vol. 14) (R. F. C. Hull, Trans.). Princeton: Princeton University Press. (Original work published 1955)

Jung, C. G. (1989). *Psychology and religion: West and east* (2nd ed., Vol. 11) (R. F. C. Hull, Trans.). Princeton: Princeton University Press. (Original work published 1958)

Jung, C. G. (1990). *Psychological types.* (Rev. ed., Vol. 6) (R. F. C. Hull, Trans.). Princeton: Princeton University Press.

Jung, C. G. (1996). *The psychology of Kundalini yoga: Notes of the seminar given in 1932 by C. G. Jung.* (S. Shamdasami, Ed.). Princeton, NJ: Princeton University Press.

Jung, C. G. (2008). *Children's dreams: Notes from the seminar given in 1936-1940.* (L. Jung & M. Meyer-Grass, Eds.) (E. Falzeder & T. Woolfson, Trans.) :Princeton: Princeton University Press. (Original work published 1987).

Jung, C.G. (2009). *The red book. (S. Shamdasani, Ed.)* (M. Kyburz, J. Peck, & S. Shamdasani, Trans.) New York: W. W. Norton & Co.

Jung, C. G. (2009). *The red book: A reader's edition.* (S. Shamdasani, Ed.) (M. Kyburz, J. Peck, & S. Shamdasani, Trans.) New York: W. W. Norton & Co.

Kant, I. (1989). In E. Hundert. *Philosophy, psychiatry, and neuroscience: Three approaches to the mind* (p. 297) Oxford: Clarendon Press.

Kryder, R. P. (1990). *Gaia Matrix Oracle* (Vol. 2). Mount Shasta, CA.: Golden Point Productions.

Loo, O. (2015). *Rapunzel 1790: A new translation of the 1790 tale.* (F. Schulz, Trans.). Charleston, SC: Loo

Mandelbrot, B. (1983). *The fractal geometry of nature.* New York: W. H. Freeman.

Meier, C. (1995). *Personality: The individuation process in the light of C. G. Jung's typology.* Einsiedeln: Daimon. (Original work published in 1977).

Myss, C. (1996). *Anatomy of the spirit: The seven stages of power and healing.* New York: Harmony Books.

Nachmanovitch, S. (1990). *Free play: Improvisation in life and art.* Los Angeles: *Jeremy P. Tarcher, Inc.*

Naifeh, S. (1995). *Archetypal foundations of addiction and recovery.* Lecture at Pacifica Graduate Institute, Winter. Carpinteria, CA.

Neumann, E. (1993). *The origins and history of consciousness.* New York: Princeton University Press. (Original work published 1949)

Ornstein R., & Swencionis, C. (Eds.). (1990). *The healing brain: A scientific reader.* New York & London: The Guilford Press.

Osserman, R. (1995). *Poetry of the universe: A mathematical exploration of the cosmos.* New York: Anchor Books. (Original work published 1884.)

Owens, L., Ed. (1981). *The complete brothers Grimm fairy tales.* New York: Crown Publishers. Inc.

Papadopoulos, R. K., Ed. (2006). *The handbook of Jungian psychology.* New York: Routledge.

Peck, C., Ed., (1998). *Treasury of North American Folktales.* New York: Quality Paperback Book Club.

Penrose, R. (1994). *Shadows of the mind: A search for the missing science of consciousness.* Oxford: Oxford University Press.

Raff, J. (2000). *Jung and the alchemical imagination.* York Beach, ME: Nicholas-Hays.

Robertson, R. (1995). *Jungian archetypes: Jung, Godel, and the history of archetypes.* York Beach, ME: Nicolas-Hays.

Robertson , R. (1997, Winter). The mote in your eye: In praise of projection. *Psychological Perspectives* (36), 92-102.

Rosa, L., Rosa, E., Sarner, L., & Barrett, S. (1998, April 1). A close look at therapeutic touch. *The Journal of the American Medical Association, 279*, 1005-1010.

Rossi, E. L. (1993). *The psychobiology of mind-body healing: New concepts of therapeutic hypnosis* (2nd ed.). New York: W. W. Norton & Company, Inc.

Rossi, E. L. (1997). The symptom path to enlightenment: The psychobiology of Jung's constructive method. *Psychological Perspectives, 36* (Winter), 68-84.

Sandford, R. (2019). *A Jungian approach to engaging our creative nature: Imagining the source of our creativity.* New York: Routledge.

Satinover, J. (1994). *The neurophysiology of traditional wisdom, psyche, synapse, & Jungian psychology in the light of modern neuroscience.* [Cassette recording series No. 540-A,B,C,D,E]. Evanston, IL: C.G. Jung Institute of Chicago.

Segal, L., Jarrell, R., & Sendak, M. (1983). *The juniper tree and other tales from Grimm.* (L. Segal & R. Jarrell, Trans.). New York: Farrar, Straus and Giroux. (Orignal work published 1973).

Shamdasani, S. (1998). *Cult fictions: C.G. Jung and the founding of analytical psychology.* New York: Routledge.

Shamdasani, S. (2003). *Jung and the making of modern psychology: The dream of a science.* Cambridge: Cambridge University Press.

Shamdasani, S. (2012). *C. G. Jung: A biography in books.* New York: W.W. Norton & Co.

Schopenhauer, A. (1995). *On the fourfold root of the principle of sufficient reason* (E.F.J. Payne, Trans.). La Salle: Open Court. (Original work published 1974).

Shannon, C., & Weaver, W. (1949). *The mathematical theory of communication.* Urbana: University of Illinois Press.

Skodol-Wilson, H. & Hutchinson, S. A. (1991). Triangulation of qualitative methods: Heideggerian hermeneutics and grounded theory. *Qualitative Health Research,* 1(2), 263-276.

Small, J. (1982). *Transformers: The therapists of the future.* Marina del Rey: DeVorss & Company.

Storr, A. (1979). *The art of psychotherapy.* London: Heinemann.

Talbot, M. (1991). *The holographic universe.* New York: Harper Collins.

Tarnas, R. (1991). *The passion of the western mind: Understanding the ideas that have shaped our world view.* New York: Crown Publishers.

Tarnas, R. (2006). *Cosmos and psyche: Intimations of a new world view.* New York: Viking Penguin.

Tatar, M., Ed. (2002). *The annotated classic fairy tales.* (M. Tatar, Trans.) London: W.W. Norton & Co.

Tatar, M., Ed. (2012). *The annotated brothers Grimm: The bicentennial edition.* (M. Tatar, Trans.). London: W. W. Norton & Co.

Van Eenwyk, J. R. (1997). *Archetypes & strange attractors: The chaotic world of symbols.* Toronto: Inner City Books.

von Franz, M. L. (1974). *Number and time: Reflections leading toward a unification of depth psychology and physics* (Andrea Dykes, Trans.). Evanston: Northwestern University Press. (Original work published in 1970).

von Franz, M. L. (1978). *Time: Rhythm and repose.* Great Britain: Thames and Hudson.

von Franz, M. L. (1980). *Alchemy: An introduction to the symbolism and psychology.* (D. Sharp, Ed.). Toronto: Inner City Books.

von Franz, M. L. (1993). *Projection and re-collection in Jungian psychology: Reflections of the soul* (W. H. Kennedy, Trans.). La Salle & London: Open Court. (Original work published 1978).

von Franz, M. L. (1995). *Shadow and evil in fairy tales.* Boston: Shambala. (Original work published 1974).

von Franz, M. L. (1996). *The interpretation of fairy tales.* Boston: Shambhala. (Original work published 1970).

von Franz, M. L. (1999). *Archetypal dimensions of the psyche.* Boston: Shambhala. (Original work published 1994).

von Franz, M. L., Ed. (2000). *Aurora consurgens: A document attributed to Thomas Aquinas on the problem of opposites in alchemy.* (R.F.C. Hull & A.S.B. Glover, Trans.). Toronto: Inner City Books.

Wilber, K. (1979). *No boundary: Eastern and Western approaches to personal growth.* Boston & London: Shambhala.

Wilber, K. (Ed.). (1985). *The holographic paradigm*. Boston & London: Shambhala.

Wilhelm, S. (1962) *The secret of the golden flower: A Chinese book of life*. (S. Wilhelm, Trans.). Orlando, FL: Harcourt Brace Jovanovich. (Original work published 1962).

Wilkins, L. E. (1995). Collaborative practice: Empowered by inner work. *Alternative* Health Practitioner, 1 (1, Spring), 73-77.

Wilkins, L. E. (1998) *A theory of transcendence based on the archetype of holography leading to a personal cosmology and the creation of the holographic mind model*. (Publication No. 3137287 [Doctoral dissertation, Pacifica Graduate Institute]. ProQuest Dissertations Publishing.

Wilkins L. E. (2002) "Metaphorical language: Seeing and hearing with the heart." *The Journal of Poetry Therapy*, (15:3 Spring). 123-130.

Zipes, J., Ed. (2014). *The complete first edition: The original folk & fairy tales of the brothers Grimm*. (J. Zipes, Trans.). Princeton, NJ: Princeton University Press.

Zipes, J., Ed. (2017). *The sorcerer's apprentice: An anthology of magical tales*. Princeton NJ: Princeton University Press.

# Index

sister, 74, 75, 76, 78, 81,
83, 88, 89, 90, 91, 92,
93, 94, 95, 96, 97, 98,
100, 102, 103, 104
six, 73, 81, 83, 98
smell, 19, 42, 62, 75, 86,
143
snake, 21
snores, 40
sons, 73, 74, 81, 82, 88,
89, 90, 91, 99, 100,
101, 104
soup, 108, 116, 121
spell, 88, 101, 102, 139,
141, 143, 153
spells, 50
spirit, 22, 29, 51, 58, 61,
69, 95, 113, 117, 125,
143, 149, 166
spirits, 54, 59
spiritual, 10, 29, 31, 50,
58, 70, 103, 151, 152,
154
Spirituality, 10, 28, 70,
104, 125, 153
Spiritually, 57
stage, 17, 45, 58, 68, 69,
70, 94, 101, 102, 118,
119, 120, 121, 124
stages, 29, 54, 97, 103,
123, 166
star, 75, 85, 87, 93, 94
stars, 75, 85, 92
stone, 3, 6, 8, 41, 129
stones, 16, 40, 69, 129

stool, 74, 85, 86, 92
structure, 1, 23, 114, 115,
124, 137, 147, 150
structures, 17, 22
sun, 38, 47, 56, 61, 75, 85,
128, 133, 140, 152
symbol, 28, 32, 51, 52, 54,
58, 65, 91, 143, 145,
146, 148, 149, 150,
151, 153
symbolic, 18, 19, 29, 45,
51, 55, 92, 146
symbolically, 56, 92, 94,
143, 147
symbolism, 9, 52, 61, 83,
84, 97, 99, 123, 139,
144, 149, 170
symbolize, 54, 55, 58, 119,
146, 147
symbolized, 59, 119
symbolizes, 124, 144, 156
symbols, 4, 9, 19, 28, 31,
59, 117, 142, 148, 164,
170
synchronicities, 4, 5
synchronicity, 4, 5
synchronistic, 4, 16
synergy, 16
Tarnas, 12, 14, 169
taste, 19, 38, 62, 143
tetrahedron, 22, 63, 95,
96, 121
three, 6, 9, 10, 26, 37, 41,
47, 50, 53, 54, 55, 58,
70, 78, 88, 89, 96, 97,

wisdom, 17, 54, 65, 66, 67, 68, 70, 88, 124, 137, 147, 168
wish, 73, 76, 81, 82, 83, 88, 103, 104, 128, 145
witch, 48, 133, 139
wolf, 37, 38, 39, 40, 41, 43, 55, 60, 65, 68
woman, 38, 40, 122, 145, 146, 162, 163
woods, 15, 37, 38, 48, 49, 53, 55, 58, 62, 64, 68, 69, 108, 117, 121
yellow, 25, 28, 69, 120
yellowing, 11, 26
yoga, 27, 28, 166

# About the Author

Lois Wilkins, PhD, APRN, is a Theorist, Depth Psychotherapist, Researcher, Consultant, and Owner of the Eagle's Nest Holistic Mental Health, Inc., in DeSoto, Kansas. She has published numerous articles and poetry. In addition to her private practice, she teaches classes, including but not limited to Fairy Tales and Dreams and Jungian Analytical/Depth Psychology.

Made in the USA
Middletown, DE
17 September 2022

10647519R00106